THE FLEXIBLE ELEMENTARY SCHOOL:
PRACTICAL GUIDELINES FOR DEVELOPING A NONGRADED PROGRAM

Evelyn M. Murray
Jane R. Wilhour

PARKER PUBLISHING COMPANY, INC.   WEST NYACK, N.Y.

© 1971, by

PARKER PUBLISHING COMPANY, INC.
West Nyack, New York

ALL RIGHTS RESERVED. NO PART OF THIS BOOK MAY BE REPRODUCED IN ANY FORM, OR BY ANY MEANS, WITHOUT PERMISSION IN WRITING FROM THE PUBLISHER.

Library of Congress
Catalog Card Number: 73-156764

PRINTED IN THE UNITED STATES OF AMERICA
ISBN - 0 - 13 - 322271 - 3
B & P

THE FLEXIBLE ELEMENTARY SCHOOL:
PRACTICAL GUIDELINES FOR DEVELOPING
A NONGRADED PROGRAM

DEDICATION

This book is dedicated to the many teachers and administrators with whom we shared ideas in the pursuit of a better education for all children.

THE CHALLENGE OF THE NONGRADED SCHOOL

We have written this book to assist teachers and administrators in implementing flexible nongraded programs in their elementary classrooms. Administrators will find essential guidelines for creating change in an entire elementary school, and the elementary teacher will secure practical curriculum suggestions, usable records and a multitude of ideas to assist her in changing from a traditional graded classroom to a flexible individualized learning environment. The authors have presented specific aspects of nongraded programs from a multitude of schools across the United States where they have worked as teachers, supervisors, and consultants to schools moving toward flexible nongraded programs. In essence, they identify schools where one can actually observe nongrading, team teaching, and individualization. A major goal of the book has been to transplant nongraded theories to the level of daily teaching procedures.

This book offers educators examples of various aspects of nongradedness, such as, flexible grouping and regrouping of children; team teaching involving large groups, small groups, and individual learning situations; independent study; individualized instruction through programmed materials and other techniques; and tutorial work by aides, student teachers, and other students.

The curriculum explained in the book will give educators planning for change in their curriculum insight for including newer trends in learning. Although, in many instances the examples illustrate the curriculum found in most elementary schools, it does depict many examples of complete individualization of instruction which is being emphasized today. Procedures for humanizing the process of education and developing positive self-concepts are also stressed in the book.

This book was written by experienced educators who have struggled through curriculum and organizational change. It will meet the needs of those who are making the transition from the graded to the nongraded school and should be helpful to those involved in various stages of readiness as well as for those who have already moved into action.

In reality, this book stems from the collective experiences of professional, experienced educators who have developed innovative nongraded programs and represents the kind of resource material essential to those who would plan better schools for a rapidly changing world.

Evelyn M. Murray
Jane R. Wilhour

ACKNOWLEDGMENTS

The materials for this book reflect the contributions of many administrators and teachers who worked with the authors as their schools moved toward more flexible programs. We would like to thank our college professors for their stimulation which prompted us to seek out better elementary school programs. Special thanks is due Russell L. Wilhour who always encouraged us to write this book. Our acknowledgments would never be complete without a special note of appreciation to our parents Mr. and Mrs. L. M. McCown and sister Beaulah, and Mr. and Mrs. C. E. Reinaker, Jr. who provided us with the opportunity to secure an undergraduate education and begin our journey into teaching. We are deeply indebted to the publishers and educators who granted us permission to use their materials. In conclusion, we acknowledge the superior cooperation and assistance provided by our publisher.

Contents

1. **Making the Change from Graded Structure to Flexible Nongraded Program** 17

   The fallacy of the graded school (19)
   Needed: new flexible organizations (22)
   The nongraded school: a framework for change in school organization (23)
   Key aspects from effective nongraded schools (25)
   Planning change: how to change from the traditional school to the nongraded organization (31)
   Summary (35)

2. **Diagnosing Children's Needs Prior to Grouping for Instruction** 37

   Planning for individualization (46)
   Considerations for teachers (48)
   Pitfalls in identifying children's needs (52)
   Summary (53)

3. **Grouping—The Basis for a Nongraded School Organization** 55

   General criteria for grouping children (56)
   Pupil placement information (59)
   How to make grouping function (59)
   Nongraded—team teaching approach, stressing individualization (67)
   Grouping and regrouping in a flexible schedule (71)
   Summary (71)

4. **Team Teaching Within the Nongraded Structure** 73

   Advantages of the team approach (73)
   Disadvantages of the team approach (75)

4. Team Teaching Within the Nongraded Structure (cont'd)... 73

Aspects of team teaching plans (76)
Staff planning (84)
Long and short range plans (87)
Model schedules for team teaching (93)
Summary (100)

5. The Curriculum in the Nongraded School 106

Professional objectives (106)
Considerations of what to teach (108)
How the content should be taught (127)
Including the scope and sequence in the curriculum (129)
Eliminating artificial subject matter divisions (130)
Organizing for instruction (131)
Role of the teacher (132)
Summary (133)

6. Utilization of Staff: A Team Approach for Planning 134

Cooperative planning (134)
The principal's role (136)
Teacher selection (137)
Teacher's responsibilities (137)
Using specialists (139)
Role and duties of teacher aides (140)
Selection of teacher aides (148)
In-service program for total staff (150)
Community resources (158)
Summary (159)

7. A Look at Reporting Practices: Continuous Evaluation of the Individual Pupil 160

Essential records (161)
Pupil placement information (161)
Personalized skill sheets (161)
Pupil progress report (173)
Parent-teacher conferences (174)

CONTENTS

7. A Look at Reporting Practices: Continuous Evaluation of the Individual Pupil (cont'd.) 160

    Transfer records (190)
    Summary (190)

8. The Materials Center: Instructional Media for the Nongraded School 193

    Services provided by the media specialists (193)
    Effective programmed material for skill development (202)
    Individualized learning kits for independent study (202)
    Computers and teaching machines (203)
    Multi-phased texts (204)
    T.V. teaching (205)
    Viewing and listening materials (206)
    Varied reference texts (209)
    Maps, globes and models; modern trade books (210)

9. Personalizing Instruction in the Nongraded School: Humanizing the Process 214

    How to motivate the learner (214)
    Prescribing the skills needed (216)
    Freeing the learner to learn on his own (217)
    Developing a self concept (218)
    Keeping the creative spark alive (220)
    Encouraging inquiry and experimentation (225)
    Working together in multi-cultural groups (226)
    Summary (228)

10. Program Evaluation and Communication 230

    Absolute essentials (230)
    Techniques used for assessing programs (234)
    Factors to be included in the evaluation (235)
    Assessing administrative change in school innovation (239)
    Persons involved in the process (244)
    Innovative programs demand excellent public relations (244)
    Summary (251)

THE FLEXIBLE ELEMENTARY SCHOOL:
PRACTICAL GUIDELINES FOR DEVELOPING
A NONGRADED PROGRAM

If you are doing something the same way you have been doing it for ten years, the chances are you are doing it wrong.

Charles Kettering

Making the Change from Graded Structure to Flexible Nongraded Program

The first chapter of the book will be devoted to the changing attitudes toward nongraded school organization. We will describe the essential factors involved and relate them directly to the administration, the school, the program, the staff, the children, and the public. We cannot overstress the significance of these steps; they are all important for changing from the traditional elementary school to the nongraded program.

Change in education is as inevitable as change in other areas of the psychological, social, physical, or economic existence of people. Therefore, it is "school people"—those who operate the schools: the board of education, the administrators, the teaching staff, and auxiliary personnel who cooperatively must shape the change. Planning change and changing the environment is the only possible way in which any school person may expect to be effective in his work. Educators who are not planning change for the best possible education for all children today are just wasting their time as well as being a hindrance to our changing society.

Since Sputnik there has been exploding interest in both improving the quality of the educational system in America and extending educational opportunities to millions of youngsters who in the past had become displaced persons in their own so-called "self-contained" classrooms. The question is: Does the self-contained classroom offer enough educational opportunity for today's youngsters who must be prepared for tomorrow's world?

As Fantini, a noted student of educational change has put it, "twice in the last ten years loud alarms have sounded about failure in education, and now the static is crackling again."[1] Further, he wondered if the nation would go to the heart of the educational matter or, as it has been doing so far, spend its energies by adding more of the same to an already outdated organization. Many share Fantini's concern that needed change is not occurring.

National concerns for education for all children have forced educators to undertake research in compensatory projects and to re-examine assumptions concerning learning and teaching. Although much of the current research has applications for *all* children in *all* schools, there are indications that the prevailing system—no matter how it is enriched—generally is not geared to the dynamic mode of the modern age, which demands life-long adaptability to swiftly changing knowledge. Moreover, the purposes of the self-contained classroom, which organized more than 150 years ago and shaped by a limited and homogeneous elementary school population, have little relevance for today's diverse elementary school population.

Hillson has called attention to the fact that the schools are now reflecting some of the fermentation of the larger society and that there is presently an impetus for finding better ways of organizing learning.[2] Not since the child-centered movement of the 1950's has there been witnessed such activity and change as that stimulated significantly during the decade of the 1960's by private foundations' support of pilot programs featuring "breakthrough" ideas.

As stated before, the self-contained elementary school which has survived for over a hundred-fifty years is caught up in a area of

---

[1] Mario D. Fantini and Gerald Weinstein, "Taking Advantage of the Disadvantaged," *Teachers College Record,* 69:103, November, 1967.

[2] Maurice Hillson, *Elementary School Reorganization: The Current Scene* (Chicago: Science Research Associates, 1966), p. 2. (Newsletter.)

MAKING THE CHANGE FROM GRADED STRUCTURE

change. Not only the American society, but the world as a whole seems to be in a state of change. The explosion of knowledge, newer technology, and the change in our social structure are crowding in on the elementary school.

Expanded knowledge concerning individual differences reveals that children differ in abilities, achievement, motivation, cultural backgrounds, and in willingness to learn.

The newer flexible buildings, varied types of instructional materials, the utilization of staff, and the advanced technology also denote that the elementary schools are changing rapidly.

This information suggests that we need different methods, materials, and organizational arrangements for different kinds of learners.

The elementary schools are not only reflecting the change noted in the changing society but also through the federal government's massive support to the innovative and exemplary programs.

Not every idea that is new or is receiving current attention should necessarily be adopted, but each deserves careful consideration before being discarded as a passing fancy. The intent of this book is (1) to review a new organizational pattern—termed "nongradedness"—that is receiving considerable attention at the present time and (2) to establish detailed guidelines designed to assist school administrators who may desire to develop a nongraded elementary school plan.

Ideas concerning change in school organization should never be borrowed, "lock, stock, and barrel." They never work in the new place which did the borrowing. Ideas about school improvement do not become good functioning plans unless there is a great deal of planning, much re-thinking, study, and preparation of the people who will carry out the plans. There must also be a steady application of the idea of flexibility. Rigid plans are never successful plans.

THE FALLACY OF THE GRADED SCHOOL

Why has the graded school failed to meet the needs of the children? Could it be its structure? The graded school structure of organization was created to (1) organize children of the same chronological age in grouping situations where pupils could progress through the schools; (2) classify content which the children would complete as they progressed through the graded structure, to group all children of the same chronological age together, assuming that all children of the same age learn the graded content at the same rate, and (3) evaluate all children of the same age by arbitrary standards for promotion, assuming that all children of the same age learn at the same rate and level. Yet, the graded structure, once established, created other factors namely: (1) graded textbooks which contained the content to be taught, (2) teacher education methods which stressed how to teach the graded content, (3) graded expectations with which teachers, pupils, and parents became acquainted, and (4) graded questions on standardized tests by which children are evaluated. Although this practice has been critized by educators and parents from the beginning, it has become a part of our culture.

Over the years, experienced and objective people have challenged, tested and disproven, to the satisfaction of many other experienced people, all of the standard assumptions about graded schools. This is not said to condemn all graded school programs or to imply that some graded schools are not "good" in the cultures in which they are operated. But, it is to say that all improvement within the graded structure and all better ways of doing things are the direct results of someone's having tested "old ways" and proven the underlying assumptions to be of doubtful value. Facts like those listed above are the kinds of understandings that prompt creative thinkers to invent new ways of doing things.

It is also worthwhile to note, at this point, that there has been no basic change in ideas about graded elementary schools during the past hundred years. As structures, graded schools have set ways of school operation. The basic concept has become completely assimilated in the minds of most people.

This criticism has been based on educational experience and observation. It soon became evident that all children of a given chronological age were not equally capable since each child has his own personal rate of growth. Many of the children in the graded school did not learn what was expected of them. The obvious answer was to have them do the work over—to repeat the grade and be labeled as a failure at the end of the year.

This has not been the answer to this educational problem. Research reveals that nongraded children achieve no more than their promoted counterparts, neither does repeating the grade enhance pupil adjustment. Studies show that promoted pupils are more accepted by others, have less disciplinary problems, and are more likely to stay in school. The content to be covered in the graded textbooks was not always effective material for the so-called "gifted" and "slow" learner, neither was it always appropriate for the child coming from a culturally deprived background. This evidence strongly indicates that the graded structure does not serve its intended purpose.

Educators have made several attempts to meet the challenge, e.g., more specialists have been hired to help supplement the classroom teacher, more of the same kind of material has been added which has increased the pressure, grouping of children in the graded classroom causing the teacher to work with a wider range of differences in abilities and interests, auxiliary personnel have been added to relieve the teachers, TV teaching has been added to help, computers, teaching machines and programmed materials have been purchased to relieve the classroom teacher. Yes, educators have continued to adjust the program to the children, but the problems still are serious ones.

In summary, we associate these facts with the more definite assumptions about graded schools. But long years of experience with graded schools show that:

1. Age alone is a poor index of pupil ability.

2. Equal "learning time" spent by different pupils of the same age produces a variety of levels of achievement.

3. The repetition of whole grades, of one school year in length, does not insure pupil progress of the same level as that attained by more able pupils during the preceding year.

4. Retarded pupils show more signs of frustration than most pupils who are not retarded.

5. Measured achievement differences between pupils of the same age and number of years of schooling vary by several years when measured at any time during their elementary school experience, etc.

6. "More of the same" material does not assure success.

During the long period of the graded structure, educators have noted that the above assumptions about graded schools are correct because children differ socially, emotionally, physically and intellectually.

NEEDED: NEW FLEXIBLE ORGANIZATIONS

It is quite apparent that the structure of the elementary graded school is not in harmony with the growth of children nor does it meet the demands of a rapidly changing society. Geared to the "so-called" average child, the graded school plan failed to make administrative provision for the individual child. The factors of differences in needs, interests, and abilities were ignored in the lockstep pattern and rigidity of the structure.

These restrictions of the graded school continued to concern educators who were attempting to individualize instruction. Educators throughout the country, as well as the federal government, and private industries have encouraged experimental programs for individualizing instruction.

When one criticizes the present self-contained classroom organization, it must be made in terms of its effectiveness for achieving the educational objectives to which the school is committed.

When deciding to change to a flexible organization, one must be mindful of the benefits and limitations. The organizational pattern is only the means to the end. It is what happens to the child in the organizational pattern that makes the difference. No organizational design is a substitute for excellence in teaching or learning. Flexible organizational approaches can make it possible for the best teacher to be more effective and for *all* children to progress at their own rate of growth. Poor organizational arrangements can reduce the effectiveness of all concerned, administrators, teachers, children, and parents.

New flexible organizations can be viewed in the light of: (1) the child—the way he learns, his interests, abilities, and needs; (2) the aims of education, based on the objectives of the school; (3) the needs of society, founded on reasonable demands; and (4) subject matter and curriculum planning—basic skills and concepts built into a curriculum which encourages individual learning styles.

The assumptions underlying the need for flexible organizational structures in the modern elementary school follow:

1. The patterns of a flexible school organization seek to differentiate progress according to the differences of children.

2. The flexible school could be designed for children to master information which could be personally identified and prescribed.

3. The flexible school could be organized so that nonpromotion disappears and no child is labeled as a "failure."

4. Flexible structures could provide for a differentiated rate of progress with variations in programs according to individual differences.

There are many possible patterns for flexible organizations for the elementary school. If the emphasis on content is blended with the desire to encourage individual differences, then modification of the graded structure is imperative. The nongraded plan as a flexible school organizational pattern warrants attention. This is the challenge of this book.

THE NONGRADED SCHOOL: A FRAMEWORK FOR CHANGE IN SCHOOL ORGANIZATION

The nongraded school seeks to solve some of the problems created by the graded structure. Yet, no matter what name we give to a new form of organization, we shall continue the graded school unless we changed graded content and graded expectations.

The nongraded school proposes a flexible structure for meeting the varied problems created by the graded structure built upon the following assumptions:

1. All children should progress at their own personal rate of growth.

2. Curriculum experiences should be differentiated to meet the needs of children.

3. Utilization of teacher talents should be developed so that children should have more challenging experiences.

4. More instructional time could be given to each child when the children are grouped in the skill subjects having a narrower range of reading and mathematics abilities.

5. Differentiation of materials for meeting the interest and achievement levels of children should motivate the learner to want to learn.

6. Flexible grouping arrangements of children should allow for large group, small group, and individual instruction.

7. The involvement of administrators, teachers, parents, and children in the planning and implementation should bring about better understanding of all concerned.

8. Evaluation appropriate to the ability of the individual child should cause better social adjustment, thus better behavior.

9. Flexible building and equipment should make it easier to personalize instruction.

10. Grouping and regrouping of children should provide opportunities for children to work and play together in biracial situations, thus learning to live together.

11. A team approach to the utilization of staff should allow for effective planning time and cooperative diagnosis of children by the staff.

The question is, how can the modern elementary school function around these assumptions? Will the nongraded school solve some of the present problems? If so, how will it be organized?

The nongraded elementary school has several possible patterns of school organization. The pattern that a school will follow will be based on the following factors: needs of the children involved, the talents of the teachers, size of the school, social and economic background of the children, type of school building, financial support from the administration and public.

The nongraded structure has several possible organizational patterns: grouping of children according to some criteron of homogeneity for certain subjects and periods of the day, or they might be grouped quite heterogeneously for some subjects or periods during the day. Furthermore, a nongraded school in its vertical pattern of organization may utilize some type of team teaching arrangement for horizontal inter-class grouping. Other plans of the nongraded school organization have completely individualized instruction in most content areas, e.g., individualized prescribed instruction, (IPI), used in the language arts and mathematics in several experimental schools, packets of content material developed in sequence for individual progression, independent study for individual projects, and programmed materials and tapes for individualizing the skill subjects.

The remainder of the chapter will discuss key aspects of five successful nongraded programs and the initial steps for change from the traditional graded school to the nongraded structure. Chapters

Two through Ten will give educators further guidelines for implementation of the nongraded program.

KEY ASPECTS FROM EFFECTIVE NONGRADED SCHOOLS

Educators initiating the nongraded program want to know how other schools have organized for instruction. Reports from five selected schools are reviewed in this portion of the chapter. These schools are located in five different states, representing different socio-economic backgrounds, and depicting multi-cultural groups. These schools range in school population from approximately four hundred to one thousand. Since the main function of the nongraded school is to individualize instruction the same guidelines are applicable to all schools whether they be located in an urban, small town, or a rural area. These schools were selected to give experienced educators essential guidelines for changing from the traditional school to flexible learning situations.

Fairview Elementary School

The staff at Fairview Elementary School, Winston Salem, North Carolina, believes that the most challenging responsibility facing us is that of providing the best teaching-learning situation possible for the boys and girls at this school.

They believe the influence of the elementary school on the child is everlasting and that the influence will serve as a foundation for all future intellectual, cultural and moral growth. Therefore, they consider it the purpose and responsibility of their school to provide an environment that will insure the maximum development of each child according to his abilities and potentialities.

OBJECTIVES

TO HELP IN FULFILLING THEIR PHILOSOPHY THEY STRIVE TO:

1. Provide an individualized learning-type environment equipped with more and improved teaching-methods, teaching aides, teaching supplies and equipment which will lead to the fullest development of all students in the acquiring of the basic learning skills.

2. Endeavor to provide experiences and develop attitudes and understandings which will alleviate feelings of insecurity and instill positive feeling toward himself and others.

3. Engage in activities and provide services which will promote good physical health, stimulate wholesome recreational and leisure-time interests and activities for wholesome living within the school environment as well as outside.

4. Bridge the gap that is prevalent between the deprived socio-economic groups and others by providing opportunities to attend fine arts programs, concerts, musicals, recitals and other aesthetic-type cultural programs—both at school and in other settings.

5. Develop an awareness of self-discipline so that pupils become better behaved and more responsible persons.

6. Aid the pupils in recognizing the social changes that confront them and help them understand how to favorably meet and react to these changes so that they might be worthy, contributing citizens to our society.[3]

McAnnulty Elementary School

Through technology and teacher-made educational materials, a few schools have been breaking the facets of education in the elementary school. One of these schools is McAnnulty School, located in the Baldwin-Whitehall Township School District in suburban Pittsburgh. The child learns mathematics, reading, and spelling at his own individual pace in one of the nation's successful operations of individualized instruction on a systematic, step-by-step basis throughout an entire school program. This four-year-old experiment has been named *Individually Prescribed Instruction.* In this school, each pupil works on his own. The second and third grade reading class, for example, use a learning center and adjoining rooms. Teachers and the school librarian act as coordinators and tutors as the pupils proceed with the various materials prepared by the school's teachers and IPI's developer, the Learning Research and Development Center at the University of Pittsburgh. Each pupil sets his own pace. When he has completed a unit of work, he is tested, the test is corrected immediately, and if he receives a grade of 85 percent or better he moves on. If the grade is lower than 85 percent,

---

[3] *A Handbook For Teachers.* Fairview Elementary School, Winston Salem, North Carolina, 1969, p. 3.

the teacher offers a series of alternative activities including special individual tutoring to correct the weaknesses. There are no prescribed textbooks. The teachers are kept busy observing the child's progress, evaluating his tests, writing prescriptions, and instructing pupils who need help individually or in small groups.

McNeill Elementary School

The school building is a single-story "E" shaped building, located in Bowling Green, Kentucky. Each wing and the rooms in the base area were divided into two separate plazas A and B. Plaza A contains personnel, materials, and equipment in four resource areas: Reading, Language Arts, Science, and Mathematics for individual students whose needs require the utilization of the rooms during the first four years of school. Plaza B has four resource areas: Language Arts, Science, Mathematics, and Social Studies containing people, places, and things for learners working in five, six, seven and eight phases of the program.

Students in the various subjects are expected to have certain common learnings, develop personal concepts and understandings, explore areas of interest, and pursue avenues of specialization as they proceed individually through the curriculum. Each student's profile in the different academic and skill areas is determined from past performance achievement and aptitude test scores, and placement in appropriate subject matter content is accompanied by designated cognition and communicative skill development activities. Mental ability scores are used as estimates of the student's potential for learning. All test results are correlated with each student's past and present learning performance to determine the *behavioral independence level*[4] a team might expect of him in academic and communication skill activities.

From these evaluations the staff develops an individualized learning program for each and every student within their particular plaza. Pupils utilize the resource areas and personnel according to the times allotted on their Learning Performance Profile Card.

Upon the completion of the period of scheduled work (Academic Package) the student is examined or tested either by a written test or

---

[4] *Behavioral Independence Level* is envisioned as the extent to which a student, with written and/or verbal instruction, may be expected to assume full responsibility for his total progress through the curriculum.

verbally. At this meeting a decision is made on the quality and quantity of the performance within the unit. If the work and expected outcomes are not satisfactory additional skill development and content study is planned with the student. Students who are successful will move into new Ac-Pacs which give even more breadth and depth in the same subject or subjects.

Planning and preparing a program for individual students in Science, Mathematics, Language Arts, and Social Studies includes all types of activities for communicative and cognitive development. There are no required number of units for students to advance to the next year's work. It is expected that some pupils will complete a few units during the year while many will finish work found to be of much greater difficulty than that usually considered appropriate for that particular age child.

Students in the school next year will be re-evaluated within a few weeks and placed in appropriate content learning and skill development activities. Some students may have regressed and be placed with less difficult materials and activities than those engaged in at the end of this current year. Other students may begin where they were the previous year and those who show increased competency and more maturity will work with much more sophisticated academic content and activities. The amount of time a pupil will spend in the skill areas is designated on the Learning Profile and he proceeds according to his ability to approach the expected level of performance.[5]

Tusculum View Elementary School

The authors served as consultants for the Tusculum View Elementary School in Greenville, Tennessee, in the initial stages of its development. The program was an outgrowth of long study by the superintendent, principal, and teachers. The following steps were taken in preparation:

1. The University of Tennessee School Planning Laboratory and other University staff members worked with the superintendent, principal, and school staff in developing the physical and instructional environment for the program.

---

[5]*Descriptive Bulletin on Operational Design of the Individualized Learning Center.* Bowling Green, Kentucky, 1967, pp. 2-4.

MAKING THE CHANGE FROM GRADED STRUCTURE

2. A majority of the staff attended a class on "Newer Trends in Education" at East Tennessee State University taught by the researcher.

3. The faculty visited nongraded schools in various sections of the United States.

4. Consultants were brought to the school for in-service workshops on the nongraded program.

5. The curricular learning sequences were outlined and revised several times to meet the needs of the children.

6. Reporting procedures including report cards, letters to parents, and conferences were used in experimental situations and were revised as needed.

7. Teaching teams were organized which included the principal, specialists, and aides.

8. Time was spent in learning how to help children work individually and in small groups.

9. The school experimented with various grouping procedures, organizing and reorganizing the grouping patterns before moving into the new school building.

The organizational plan, as observed by the authors and explained by the faculty, was based on the belief that students develop and progress at different rates throughout the educational process. In the purest form of this organization, a student was admitted to the program when he was ready, regardless of age. The student who began in the nongraded program was able to progress through the first six or seven years of formal education in a smooth, continuous manner. There was no passing, failing, or repeating work previously learned. Completion of the elementary portion of the educational experience was based on the basic skills felt to be necessary in order to achieve success in the nongraded junior high program in Greenville.

The students at Tusculum View were grouped both homogeneously and heterogenously. They were grouped heterogeneously for administrative purposes in science and social studies. They were grouped and regrouped homogeneously for arithmetic and language arts. According to the principal, the assignment of students to the most appropriate work groups in each area became quite a task. The teacher, principal, and team leaders considered the specific needs of students—age, achievement, ability, aptitude, social and emotional maturity, physical development, and sex. In some cases the services of the speech therapist, school nurse, school guidance personnel, social worker, and school psychologist were necessary.

The nongraded program does not lend itself to rigid scheduling. Therefore, the modules of time method was utilized at Tusculum View. The schedule was divided into fifteen-minute modules. The number of modules assigned each part of the curriculum was determined by the individual needs of the children. This was on a weekly basis of 135 modules. Movement from one area to another was made according to the needs of the individual student. The student was responsible for meeting his own appointments.[6]

Harris School

The St. Charles, Missouri School System through an ESEA, Title III grant nongraded six of its eight elementary schools. Each school devised a unique plan to most effectively meet the needs of the children it serves.

Harris Elementary School made significant beginning progress in nongrading the language arts and mathematics programs. It is important to note that this progress was due to the cooperative effort of the principal and teachers in planning the program. The principal posed many ideas about nongrading in informal discussions with individual teachers, "coffee klatch" discussions in the teachers lounge, and formal faculty meetings. As a united faculty they then chose to make preparations for nongraded organizational implementation.

The faculty devised a levels plan in years one through six for language arts and mathematics. Children were placed in homogeneous groups for language arts according to achievement level and teacher judgment. Regrouping according to the same critieria was employed for mathematics placement. Detailed skill sheets were written by the teachers to accompany each level in language arts and mathematics.

This program is distinctive for its high degree of principal-faculty participation in planning and implementation, as well as for its thorough development of levels and skill sheets.

---

[6] Bulletin: Tusculum View Elementary School, Greenville, Tennessee. 1968. pp. 3-4.

PLANNING CHANGE: HOW TO CHANGE FROM THE TRADITIONAL SCHOOL TO THE NONGRADED ORGANIZATION

The successful establishment of a nongraded elementary school worthy of the name may be considered a major accomplishment. The best and most durable of nongraded programs show that they are the end product of careful planning, enthusiasm, determination, and experience. The suggestions offered in this section for planning and initiating the nongraded school should be helpful to schools or school systems which are in the very early stages of nongraded program development.

No two nongraded programs are likely to have precisely the same organizational pattern. Factors such as size and socio-economic conditions of the community, enrollment and location of the school, and characteristics of the school population will tend to influence the course of the program's development. A detailed plan of organization which is to be followed by any school or school system must be devised by the staff whose commitment to the plan is essential to its implementation. In general, however, initial steps in program development by schools or school systems should be based in part upon generalizations drawn from broad study and observation. They should also take into account specific educational objectives and the needs of the children.

Consistency of purpose is necessary but the exact definition of the purpose of change need not be the same for all concerned. Yet, any change decided upon must be supported by the school staff and supporting school community if it is to be effective.

Broad Base of Cooperation in Planning

As stated before, any important recommendation for those developing nongraded programs is that the base of cooperative support for the program be made as broad as possible. Planning should involve the administrative staff, teachers, aides, specialists, and other school personnel regardless of the roles they will play in the established program. Parents and children should also take appropriate parts in planning the program. The wider the base of persons sensibly and purposefully involved in planning and organizing the program, the greater its chances for success. Lack of meaningful planning by all individuals to be involved may cause the program to lack the real substance of changed pupil, teacher, and parent behavior which the nongraded school seeks to accomplish. The board of education, superintendent, supervisor, principal, and faculty all have large and important roles in planning the new organization. The effective work of all of these people is extremely necessary in the establishment of an excellent nongraded school program.

Chief among the problems of the planners is the formulation of new policies based on the basic philosophy of the school system. These must be presented to the board of education for approval. The policies must be drawn (1) to guide principals, teachers, and parents to a conviction of the value of the program, (2) to provide for in-service education for principals and teachers, (3) to provide for the use of a variety of teaching aids and materials for each school and each level, and (4) to provide for progress reports to be sent home based entirely upon the concept of "continuous progress."

Fixing Responsibility

If the program is to be successful, it is recommended that overall responsibility for its development be assigned to a person who is thoroughly knowledgeable with regard to the nongraded elementary school program; this must be the principal or a curriculum coordinator. Responsibility cannot be divided equally among supervisors, department heads, and principals. Accountability for the program must be the function of individuals whose primary responsibility is the nongraded program.

Knowledge of Nongraded Programs

Innovators of the nongraded school must be acquainted with the operation of the nongraded school and must know how to communicate their knowledge to teachers, parents, school board members, and the public.

The background preparation for those who would organize nongraded schools is a thorough study of the literature in the field. While research has not yet provided final answers to all questions concerning nongraded schools, it has furnished innovators with a great deal of useful information and reasoned argument. Colleges and universities are generally most cooperative in providing assistance to teachers and administrators who are interested in improving their school programs. College courses providing insights into contemplated changes should be utilized to the fullest extent, especially those which can be tailored to provide the information needed to make a smooth organizational transition.

It is important that those involved in the program visit other nongraded schools to observe the children at work and to talk with the principals and teachers concerning their programs.

In addition to knowing the literature and how successful nongraded programs work, administrators must know the facts about their own school system and community; for example, the number of gifted students, the number of underachievers, those in need of remedial instruction, and those belonging in special classes needing specialized help.

Workshops dealing with curriculum materials, grouping procedures, public relations, testing, and evaluation should be held to clarify aims and purposes of the contemplated innovations. The services of experienced and knowledgeable consultants have proved to be a worthwhile investment. The consultants can assist in planning and organizing and can help less experienced school personnel to avoid many pitfalls.

The following is an outline of an in-service workshop held for Washington County Schools in Abingdon, Virginia, before initiating the nongraded program enabling the staff to become acquainted with the essential procedures for nongrading elementary schools.

In-Service Education Program, Abingdon, Virginia

Topic	Method of Study
1. Need for Organizational Change with Basic Orientation Regarding the Special Problems of Culturally Diverse Youth	Consultants, films, discussions
2. Schools Currently Involved in New Organizational Approaches	Consultants and films

3. Child Development and Its Implications for New Organizational Approaches with Emphasis on Culturally Diverse Children and Kindergarten Education — Consultants, discussions

4. Operational Theory: Graded Schools and New Organizational Approaches — Consultants and discussion

5. Initial Procedures in Changing from Graded Schools to Newer Organizational Approaches — Panel of consultants who have been involved in organizational change; discussion

6. Techniques for Pupil Identification and Placement — Consultants—counseling, testing guidance
   (a) Family background
   (b) Environment
   (c) Income in homes
   (d) Emotional problems
   (e) Agencies in community
   (f) Tests
   (g) School records
   (h) Observation

7. Organizational Variations in Newer Educational Approaches — Consultants, films, filmstrips, field trips, demonstrations, reports, and discussions
   (a) Team teaching
   (b) Ungraded schools
   (c) Cross-class grouping
   (d) Specialization
   (e) Independant study
   (f) Programmed learning
   (g) Language arts blocks
   (h) Partial grouping
   (i) Grouping for remedial work
   (j) Summer enrichment programs
   (k) Grouping with the use of aides and specialists
   (l) Newer content (modern mathematics, the linguistic approach in language arts, the experience approach to writing)

8. Appropriate Installation and Development of Newly Formulated Plans
   (a) Role of the supervisor
   (b) Role of the teacher
   (c) Role of the parent
   (d) Role of the student
   (e) Role of the others, including aides, specialists

   Consultants, films, and discussions

9. Evaluation of Plans
   (a) Variety of tests
   (b) Opinions of teachers, students, and parents
   (c) Evaluative instruments

   Consultants and group work

SUMMARY

In summary, change in education is inevitable. Therefore, it is the school people, those who operate the schools, that must make the change. Since change causes conflict, it takes creative plans to bring people together to think and act. Change must be supported by the school staff and the supporting people.

Planning should involve the administrative staff, teachers, aides, specialists, and other school personnel regardless of the roles they will play in the established program. The wider the base of those involved in the planning and organizing of the program, the greater are the chances of success for the nongraded school.

Initial steps in program development by schools and for school systems should be based in part upon generalizations drawn from broad study and observation. They should also take into account specific educational objectives and the needs of the children. These objectives must be based upon sound theory, general objectives of education, and they must also make provision for the accommodations of individual differences. The objectives should be written so they can later be tested, thus providing the basis for future evaluation.

Other essential steps to follow in implementing nongraded programs follow: (1) become knowledgeable concerning the philosophy of the nongraded school, (2) know the facts about the school or school system involved in the change, (3) involve all persons concerned with the program in in-service education, e.g., visitation, college classes, workshops, and faculty meetings, and (4) include the parents and community in the orientation toward the program. The above considerations are basic essentials for "Change in the Making" from the graded structure to the nongraded program.

2

Every man who knows how to read has it in his power to magnify himself, to multiply the ways in which he exists, to make his life full, significant and interesting.

Aldous Huxley

Diagnosing Children's Needs
Prior to Grouping for Instruction

One of the major goals of the flexible elementary school is to provide children with the opportunity to progress at their own rate. If this goal is to be accomplished you, the teacher, must develop diagnostic teaching skills. In order to encourage children to work at their own rate one must discover their strengths and weaknesses in many areas, and then prescribe a program designed to capitalize on these strengths and improve the areas of weakness. Obviously this diagnosis cannot be accomplished in a day or a week but each daily classroom situation can provide you with more information about a child until accumulated data will begin to give you an adequate basis for grouping and individualizing instruction.

First, you will find it helpful to design a diagnostic information data sheet similar to the model shown on page 38.

DIAGNOSTIC INFORMATION SHEET

Name _____

Age _____

Year in School _____

INTELLIGENCE TEST SCORES

Date
Administ-   *Name of Test*   *I.Q. Score*   *Mental Age*
tered

ACHIEVEMENT TEST SCORES

Date   *Name*
Administ-   *of*   *Reading*   *Skills*   *Comprehension*   *Math*   *Social*
tered   *Test*   *Studies*

OBSERVATIONS OF CHILD'S SCHOOL BEHAVIOR

Date   *Behavior*   *Conditions Under which It Occurred*

MEDICAL INFORMATION

Specific Health Problems

SPECIAL TALENTS, ABILITIES, OR CONTRIBUTIONS

Date   *Teacher*

DIAGNOSING CHILDREN'S NEEDS

The recorded information on the aforementioned model should follow the child throughout his school career so that each teacher may learn about the child from it and contribute further information which she will gain while teaching the child.

Observations

Observations of a child's behavior in specific situations will be a great asset in determining the child's reactions to given situations. This particular portion of the data sheet deserves much thought and very objective recording. When observations are properly carried out and recorded they are an invaluable technique for diagnosing children's needs and capabilities. This specific portion of the sheet may be added to so that by the time a child reaches his sixth year in school there may be five or six additional pages describing the child's behavior in selected situations. Naturally this also provides you, the teacher, with a valuable record of the child's progress or lack of it during his elementary school career in selected situations.

Essentially the data sheet is a place to record information about a child which will help you teach him more effectively and provide an opportunity for him to learn at his own rate. It is obvious that achievement test and intelligence test information will be secured either by the teacher or school psychologist administering, scoring and interpreting the tests.

Check Sheets

Another means of obtaining information about the child's immediate level of performance is through the utilization of a check sheet developed by the kindergarten teachers at Harris School in St. Charles, Missouri. As will be noted, the teachers not only learn from the information themselves but inform parents of the child's level of performance in order that they may encourage the child at home. It is most worthwhile to observe that they are using a diagnostic technique in a dual manner. Their plan could be adapted and utilized at any grade level in practically any subject area. The authors of this book would be most interested in hearing about any adaptations which teachers might make of these check sheets.

HARRIS ELEMENTARY SCHOOL
1025 Country Club Rd.   723-3448
St. Charles, Missouri   63301

Dear Parents,

The school year has reached the halfway point and I am sure many of you are interested to know how your child is progressing thus far.

Since the kindergarten does not give "grade cards" as the upper levels do, we wish to inform you of your childs' progress through this letter.

The kindergarten year is a big adjustment for some children. Many children have never been away from home for any period of time before. We have a few children who do need a little more time to "grow" before they are really ready to begin formal skill work. We believe, in keeping with the philosophy of the ungraded system, that children are individuals and need to develop at their own rate.

If your child is having some difficulty with a certain skill area, you will find attached to this letter the *skill* and some suggestions you can use at home to help your child strengthen this skill.

We are very happy to say that the children are interested in learning and have been a pleasure to work with.

If at any time you have a question please contact us for an appointment.

_____Your child is working satisfactorily.

_____Your child could use some review in the skill area attached but is otherwise doing satisfactorily.

_____Listening habits need to be improved.

LEARNING COLOR NAMES

Have your child:

1. Name colors of cars you pass when driving to the store.

2. Comment on the colors she's wearing—
    EXAMPLE: "wear your *green* dress to school."

DIAGNOSING CHILDREN'S NEEDS 41

3. When coloring, see if he/she can tell you the colors he's used.

4. Games they can play:

   Winnie The Pooh
   Candyland
   Choo-Choo Train

5. Discuss colors of things around the house and outdoors.

NUMBER READINESS

1. Count objects such as the number of forks needed to set the table, number of napkins; how many chairs are at the table, etc. Anything tangible he can count.

2. Make a set of number cards (4" x 4" cardboard squares with numerals 1–10) This set of cards can be used for many activities.

   a. have child read numeral and bounce a ball, jump, clap, etc. that many times.
   b. sort cards in numerical order.
   c. take one card out and see if he can figure out which one is missing.

3. Bingo is a good game for recognition of numerals. It is best to make your own set of cards so they aren't too difficult.

4. *Discuss shapes of things*—Square, circle, triangle, rectangle. Example: What shape is our table, doors, windows, etc.

5. Dominoes help children recognize number groups.

Self-Evaluation

It is vital for the teacher to understand how the child views his performance in school, if she is to know where he is insecure and other areas in the curriculum where he is quite confident and relaxed. When the teacher has gained this information she is more able to provide assurances and challenges at the opportune time. The self-evaluation form may sometimes be an effective basis for discussion in individual conferences. The following form is a sample of the type of self-evaluation a child can complete after appropriate directions have been given by the teacher. The child must be assured

HARRIS ELEMENTARY SCHOOL
St. Charles, Missouri
Kindergarten Skill Sheet

Name of Child _____ Month _____

Skill Areas		1	2	3	4	5	6	7	8	9
Listens										
Follows directions										
Self-expression										
Knows name										
Knows address										
Knows phone number										
Can run										
Can skip										
Can hop										
Can tie shoes										
Can tie head scarf										
Can zip										
Can button										
Is co-operative										
Is responsible/dependable										
Has self-confidence										
Is shy										
Is EASILY upset										
Is aggressive										
Recognizes & names	circle									
	square									
	triangle									
	rectangle									
Recognizes & Names	purple									
	yellow									
	brown									
	red									
	black									
	green									
	blue									
	orange									

COMMENTS:

DIAGNOSING CHILDREN'S NEEDS

KINDERGARTEN SKILL SHEET - 2

Name _____   Month

	1	2	3	4	5	6	7	8	9
Hears rhyming sounds									
Hears beginning consonant sounds									
Recognizes printed name									
Names letters in name									
Can count orally 1 - 10									
Understands 1st-5th									
Understands one to one correspondence									
Can identify numerals 1 - 10									
Can reproduce numerals 1 - 10									
Names days of week									
Understands today yesterday tomorrow									
Tells story in proper sequence									
Sees likenesses & differences left-right									
Know directions top-bottom									

Test results _____   Date _____

Teacher _____

that the form will be kept confidential and that he should answer it as honestly as possible.

Diagnostic Tests

Many teachers find it to their advantage to develop diagnostic tests for their immediate teaching level. When all teachers in the school do this it is possible to number and code the tests to be kept in a central file where teachers have access to them. The tests are usually short ten or fifteen minute tests designed to ascertain if a child has mastered a specific skill such as the subtraction facts in arithmetic or the short vowels in reading. A short diagnostic measure of this type can provide the teacher with immediate objective information about a child's level of performance. This information combined with other accumulated data and daily teacher observation of the child enables the teacher to make assignments that permit the child to work at his own pace. It is essential that the teacher record on the form shown on page 45 each diagnostic test which the child has taken so other team teachers and future teachers will know his performance level in a particular skill. The authors note that many teachers develop these tests for their own room only and do a most effective job of

SELF EVALUATION

	I would like to do extra work	I am making progress	I need help	Comments
Reading				
Spelling				
Arithmetic				
Art				
Music				

Please write a paragraph to describe the way you view your progress so far this year.

DIAGNOSING CHILDREN'S NEEDS

DIAGNOSTIC TEST INFORMATION PROFILE

Name _____ School Term _____

Age _____ _____

Year in School _____ _____

	Reading				*Mathematics*		
Test Number	Date Administered	*Score* Right	Wrong	Test Number	Date Administered	*Score* Right	Wrong
1	1/16	14	1	12	12/7	18	2
2	1/20	6	4	13	12/10	10	1
3	2/5	3	3	17	12/18	9	1
4	2/9	10	0	22	12/20	17	1
5	2/15	9	1	24	1/5	7	3
6	2/20	14	1	30	1/13	15	0
7	3/5	7	3	31	1/28	4	6
8	3/7	15	0	38	2/3	8	2
9	3/18	9	1	40	2/27	15	0
10	4/1	20	0	42	3/11	10	0
11	4/6	13	2	42	3/22	17	3
12	4/8	19	1	46	3/30	8	2
13	4/15	19	1	48	4/4	15	-
14	4/21	10	0	50	4/13	9	1
15	5/2	10	0	51	4/29	8	2
16	5/4	15	1	53	5/6	20	0
17	5/10	17	3	54	5/9	19	1

diagnosing children's mastery levels. It is obvious that if this is eventually done throughout the school there will be more continuity to the program and even greater benefits for the children.

PLANNING FOR INDIVIDUALIZATION

As we are diagnosing children's strengths and weaknesses it quickly becomes apparent that you must begin to plan and organize the classroom for individualized instruction. Naturally, there are no easy ways to approach this task, but the following guidelines may give you some direction as you attempt to discover the most appropriate organizational plan for your individual classroom. The authors have utilized these guidelines in their own elementary classrooms and found them to be a good basis for moving toward individualized instructional practices. As is true with most guidelines they will be utilized best when you adapt them to your unique classroom situation, and remember only you can decide what will be most effective for you and your students because you know them better than any other educator.

1. Study school plans for individualization

    a. Write to schools utilizing individualization in order to secure descriptions of their plans
    b. Observe in individualized classrooms
    c. Review the literature on individualization

2. Develop the plan most suitable for your students and classroom

3. Devise effective records and forms necessary for recording student progress and directing student work

ORGANIZING FOR INDIVIDUALIZED INSTRUCTION

1. Be sure classroom policies and procedures are firmly established

2. Introduce the concept of individualized instruction to the entire class

    a. Explain the specific area which will be individualized
    b. Tell the class what will be expected of them in the way of any new classroom regulations

DIAGNOSING CHILDREN'S NEEDS

c. Ask the students for their reactions to the individualized plan, and give them the opportunity to offer additional suggestions and revisions

3. Begin the new program at the beginning of a week. Work very *slowly* in the first week and establish the program on a firm foundation

Monday — Provide a short review of the new program. Then launch it.

Tuesday — Talk with the group in terms of an initial evaluation of Monday's experience. Stress the positive points first— *Then* move to the areas where improvements must be made. Now, work through the second period of individualized instruction.

Wednesday — Proceed with the program and make needed adjustments

Thursday — Proceed with the program. At this point it should begin to run smoothly

Friday — At the close of the individualized period, evaluate the week's progress with the class.

Later, as a teacher, individually evaluate your program.

Proceed with the program and make improvements and adjustments as they are needed.

Child's Individual Weekly Assignments

Many teachers find it beneficial to use a form similar to the one shown on page 49 for each child's individual assignments. General group assignments are also sometimes noted so that the child knows what activities to prepare for in a week such as a science fair as indicated on the sample assignment sheet.

The form shown on page 50 may be posted in the classroom to indicate specific assignments on selected dates. This enables the child to begin math when he chooses. It also provides the teacher with a short outline of what each child is doing at a given time in math.

The class record would list each of the thirty or thirty-five children in the class. In order to conserve space a sample of only nine children's assignments is illustrated here.

CONSIDERATIONS FOR TEACHERS

THE GIFTED, DISADVANTAGED AND UNDERACHIEVERS

There are three major categories of children that we must consider as we group children through diagnostic teaching: (1) Children who are gifted, (2) children who are disadvantaged and (3) children who are underachievers. It must be immediately borne in mind that these terms are used so that we may talk about three broad categories that children may fall into in one subject area but not in another. For example, a child may be gifted in science abilities and talents, but an underachiever in mathematics and actually disadvantaged in art and music simply due to lack of experience and exposure in these fields. Let us remember then if we identify a child as being in one of these categories in a specific subject field he will not necessarily be in that same category in all other curriculum areas. It is agreed that a child can conceivably be gifted in every subject area or disadvantaged in all areas but this is usually the exception rather than the rule, and we must keep this thought constantly before us to perform the best diagnosis of needs, and ultimately the most effective teaching, for each individual.

Let us stop and consider ourselves for a moment. Can we truly say we are in no way disadvantaged? Are there not times when we might be considered a part of a disadvantaged group due to lack of opportunity and experience? As we think about this the authors are immediately reminded of the great impact a priest had on them when in a group discussion he pointed out that an individual who had not experienced love between a man and woman such as himself had a type of deprivation. We use this example to illustrate how important it is to realize that there is not one among us who is not disadvantaged in some manner. The same thing is true of children and it is important for us to realize that probably at some time in specific subject areas a child will be gifted and at another time in a different field he may be an underachiever.

As we think about these categories in identifying children's needs and grouping them for instruction it is helpful to review the following types of activities which may be most beneficial for the gifted, the disadvantaged or the underachiever. The activities lists are mainly presented to cause you to think about how you can adapt them and add to them in your particular classroom.

INDIVIDUAL WEEKLY ASSIGNMENTS

Student's Name _____ Week beginning _____

SUBJECT	Monday	Tuesday	Wednesday	Thursday	Friday	Comments
Reading 9:00-11:00	Workbook p. 15, 16 --------- * 10:30-10:50	Attend skill group lesson on prefixes	Workbook p. 17, 18 19	Group Assignment on board --------- Library	Write a story and draw pictures for it	
Math 11:00-12:00					*11:15-11:30	
Spelling 1:00-1:20		Unit 11 - Part A — Add five new words to your individualized spelling list.			Final Test on Unit 11 & new list	
Handwriting 1:25-1:40		Write a story using new spelling words	Select the letters that are most difficult for you.			
Science 2:00-2:30		Class orientation about science fair projects	Time to work on science fair projects at school.		Field trip to Science Fair Field Trip	
Social Studies 2:30-3:00		Class Presentation			Field Trip	
Student Initiated Independent Project 2:30-3:30			To be filled out by the student			

*Student and Teacher Conference

CLASS RECORD FOR INDIVIDUALIZED SUBJECT AREA

Date	4-2	4-3	4-4	
John	Workbook p. 16		Conference	
Marilyn	Individual Packet	Skill Group	Test	
Lillian	Skill Group			
Todd	Conference			
Ken	Math Text p. 25	Test		
Betty	Math Test			
Russell	Math Test			
Janice	Worksheet No. 15			
Pam	Book p. 12			

ACTIVITIES FOR THE GIFTED

1. Tutoring

2. Discussion, Group Leaders

3. Designing small curriculum units and helping to teach them

4. Participating in or organizing local crusades against pollution or drugs by writing stories—designing commericals

5. Making tapes

6. Pursuing independently an academic area of special interest by programmed instruction, extension, or television

7. Writing stories, plays, poetry, for use in class or for school wide presentation

8. Dramatizing original writings

9. Participating in or leading brainstorming groups

DIAGNOSING CHILDREN'S NEEDS

10. Designing new games for fun and instructional purposes

11. Describe an article inside and outside

12. Writing radio announcements

13. Designing commericals for radio, television and the newspaper

ACTIVITIES FOR THE DISADVANTAGED

1. Field trips in and around the community to acquaint the child with his environment

2. Doing school work orally by talking into a recorder; thus eliminating the need for writing in his early school career

3. Providing the child with many concrete materials so that he will not be placed in the position of having to cope with ideas and problems he has never experienced

4. Use of the abacus in mathematics

5. Developing an understanding of math concepts through the use of Cuisinaire rods

6. Learning to brainstorm on his level

7. Panel discussions

8. Dramatization

9. Planning and making murals

10. Make a list of questions you want answered and then proceed to answer them

ACTIVITIES FOR THE UNDERACHIEVER

1. Recording or writing stories about his own experiences and ideas to encourage his interest and enable the teacher to discover ways of motivating him at school

2. Development of brainstorming abilities in small class groups

3. Providing them with topics to write about such as:

   What if I were a spaceman?
   What do you wonder about?
   I feel proud when.....
   I feel bad when.....
   I wish people wouldn't.....

4. Puppet Shows

5. Giving him the opportunity to plan a half day or a full day at school exactly as he would like it to be and then permitting him to carry it out so far as practical and feasible

6. Preparation of a book jacket

7. Develop a sales talk and present it to the class

8. Preparing a song or a dance for the class to enjoy at recess

9. Making a game out of the arithmetic facts through the nines and giving it to children in the primary grades

While it is always obvious that an underachiever or a disadvantaged child in a particular academic area has many problems it is frequently not noted what strengths he may have and it is here that we teachers often make a great mistake as we should learn to recognize their strengths and capitalize on them while at the same time trying to improve a weakness. Many times it is possible to bring about improvement of a problem if it is approached through a strength the child may exhibit.

In conclusion let us stress once more that no child should be identified in one of these three major categories and remain there forever. This is not diagnostic teaching or good utilization of the information secured about a child.

PITFALLS IN IDENTIFYING CHILDREN'S NEEDS

Naturally, there are pitfalls in identifying children's academic needs. You will find it is valuable to consider the following guidelines when diagnosing children's capabilities and identifying instructional patterns for them.

DIAGNOSING CHILDREN'S NEEDS

1. Remember that all groups are flexible and children should be able to move in and out of them when the group is no longer working in an area where a child needs help.

2. Movement in and out of groups is decided by the teacher on the basis of available diagnostic data.

3. No one diagnostic tool will give you adequate information; rather each technique contributes to the overall profile.

4. Recognize that you will make mistakes in diagnosing and grouping and always be ready to make a change if you see an error has been made.

5. Children change rapidly at times and vary slowly at other times and you need to be aware of the child's immediate growth pattern to teach him most effectively.

6. All diagnostic information is to be considered confidential.

7. A variety of teacher opinions and observations of a child will present a more complete picture of the child.

8. Utilize any information you can gain from the parents through conferences or written materials.

9. Be cognizant of the child's social growth and acceptance by his peers.

10. Enlist the help of a school counselor for problem cases whenever possible.

It is hoped that these guidelines will help you to avoid some of the pitfalls teachers have experienced in the past as they tried to identify children for grouping and instructional purposes.

SUMMARY

After thinking about nongraded school organization and reading about diagnostic teaching it becomes apparent that it is impossible to attain true nongrading without providing for individual differences in instruction. A review of this chapter provides you with many ideas for adopting and adapting diagnostic techniques in your classroom.

You must remember that each teacher and/or school system will determine the tools and techniques which will enhance their particular school program. For optimum implementation of diagnostic procedures the teachers must be actively involved in the planning and utilization of these devices.

The common good of a group is a social aim of democracy. A proper balance should be maintained between the development of the independent individual and the social individual.

*William Burton
Phi Delta Kappan*

Grouping—The Basis for a Nongraded School Organization

A nongraded program demands flexibility for grouping the children. The graded structure is too standardized to meet the individual differences of children. Children are different, therefore, groupings whether they be large, small, or individual must be based upon the needs of children. Teachers, too, are different and should be assigned to groups according to their abilities and interests.

To come to grips with things as they are, we must first convince ourselves that individual differences in learning ability among children do exist. Next, we need to deal with them in the school. Grouping may be a part of the answer, although no grouping unless it be directed toward individualization should be considered.

The nongraded school endeavors to meet the challenge; radical departures from the customary conventional school characterize the organizational procedures of the nongraded school. Procedures which govern the development of each child and teacher and which control the rate of student movement through the nongraded sequence must be related to the abilities, interests, talents, and needs of the pupils. If the potential advantages of the nongraded type of elementary school program are to be realized they will necessarily flow from astute and flexible grouping of children for instructional purposes.

Yes, grouping is unavoidable. Whenever there are two or more people to be taught, the differences between them become apparent. If they are to be taught "the same thing," a difference in teaching method must be devised to accomplish the purpose. If, on the other hand, the judgment of those who teach, or the purposes of those to be taught, decree that they be taught different things, there must be some arrangement to accomplish these purposes. That is, individual differences in pupils, the numbers to be taught, the purposes of the school program, and the limitations of "one" teacher all combine into the reasons for grouping. And, grouping for teaching exists in every school; even when the grouping is no more complicated than that resultant from the happenstance of birth dates.

GENERAL CRITERIA FOR GROUPING CHILDREN

There can be no satisfactory criteria for grouping the pupils in nongraded schools unless the purposes of that school are well-defined and fully understood as working principles. There is no reason for grouping except as a possible means to accomplish the purposes for which the school exists. Since the accomplishment of any school purpose is an individual and personal thing, so too, the reasons for grouping are also individual and personal. In every instance, the criteria actually used will reflect some purpose or purposes. If these purposes are other than those of the school program, then, they are not a satisfactory basis for grouping.

Criteria, as used here, are not to be confused with standards. Though these two words are sometimes used synonymously, they do not mean the same thing. The idea in the word criterion is that of a basis (or bases) of judgment. A criterion implies a test or rule of measurement. It may, and usually does indicate intent, but it does not indicate, or set, a fixed amount of anything; as is the case with a standard.

GROUPING

In grouping, the purpose of using criteria, as opposed to standards, is to allow for the flexibility of judgment that is always necessary when human beings are concerned. Grouping is a "whole process" not an incidental activity to be necessarily based upon fixed ideas. Rather, it should be an effort to consider as many possible factors of the whole situation as possible. Since the purposes of grouping are all human purposes, the following suggested bases of judgment are intended to be simple indications of the kinds of concerns to be resolved when pupils are grouped for instruction. However, it is felt that these, and perhaps many other factors, should be considered in all efforts to group pupils for instruction and/or learning activities, especially in a nongraded school program.

Many people working in education tend to avoid the broad and complicated aspects of decision-making when it comes to grouping students. The general and historical tendency, possibly tied to the "scientific movement" in education, has been to use all manner of "easy" categories for grouping—*black and white situations called standards; all of which establish fixed cut-off points.* Age grouping may be described in birth dates, which is a variety of heterogeneous grouping. There are all sorts of homogeneous groupings, based on any sort of "measurement" such as intelligence, reading levels, general ability, grouping by sex, grouping based on natural association, et cetera. All of these, perhaps, have their place and there are times when they may, as single methods of categorization, "do the job." But, it seems more than likely that any single "standard," or criterion, for that matter, is too narrow a basis for the best in grouping. No single standard can possibly reflect more than one of the purposes of the school in which the grouping is to be done.

The idea that is intended to be reflected by the kinds of criteria suggested here is that any and all grouping should be done with "the whole child" and the "whole school program" clearly in mind. If the purposes of the school are well understood by the people doing the grouping, and if they are seriously applied in the process of determining the criteria, many factors will automatically be considered and *"cut-off"* points will be *flexible* within whatever bounds *the total of the school purposes seem to indicate.*

We turn now to a suggested list of criteria for grouping in a nongraded school. This listing is representative of the kinds of things to be considered when any group is formed. It is not intended or supposed to be entirely adequate or even comprehensive in terms of the purposes of any particular school. Rather, it should suggest that there is far more to *good grouping* than the establishment of a few arbitrary cut-off points of the type so very common and here referred to as methods of "easy categorization."

Some basic general criteria for grouping children so as to assure attainment of the objectives of the nongraded elementary school program follow:

1. The grouping procedures should tend to increase pupil participation in learning activities such as (a) problem-solving, (b) critical and creative thinking, (c) dramatic participation, (d) concept development, (e) self-discipline, and (f) skill development in language arts, mathematics, and social attitudes.

2. The grouping procedures should make possible learning situations that are (a) appropriate to the pupil's general ability and achievement, (b) appropriate to the tasks the child is expected to perform as well as his psychological make-up, and (c) rewarding to the pupil.

3. The grouping procedures should tend to fulfill such general curriculum purposes as (a) combining of subject matter areas, (b) independent study, (c) research-centered projects, and (d) pupil specialization.

4. The grouping procedures should fulfill such particular subject matter purposes as (a) skill development appropriate to the need, (b) use and understanding of concepts, (c) explanation and discovery, (d) experimentation, (e) construction, and (f) viewing and listening.

5. The grouping procedures should contribute to (a) effective use of teacher talents, (b) staff and auxiliary personnel cooperation, and (c) use of a wide variety of teaching methods and materials.

6. The suggested grouping procedures should take account of available resources of space and time such as (a) space for large groups, small groups, and individual work; (b) time for the instructional task to be accomplished; (c) location of instructional materials; and (d) time and space for planning and preparing for group activities.

When these general criteria for grouping are observed, an organizational pattern and organizational procedures different from those of the traditional graded school will inevitably emerge. This pattern will provide for continuous, unbroken, upward progression for all

GROUPING

learners, with due recognition of the wide variability of learners in every aspect of their development.

PUPIL PLACEMENT INFORMATION

Children are placed in the nongraded school by various methods. They are grouped on the basis of chronological ages, interests, social characteristics, personality, sex, achievement, and other factors concerning child growth and development.

Placement in grouping will be based on individual achievement, interest, talents, and other competencies as well as deficiencies.

Consideration will be given to the chronological age of children in order that placement will not lead to social maladjustment. Factors taken into consideration for placement should include:

1. Achievement

2. I. Q.

3. Age

4. Social Characteristics

5. Personality

6. Emotional Stability

7. Teacher Opinion

8. Other Related Factors

The Pupil Placement Information Form on page 60 is for placing children in appropriate groups for instruction.

HOW TO MAKE GROUPING FUNCTION

If the recommended criteria are to be translated into effective practice, various types of grouping techniques are mandatory in the nongraded elementary school. As was made clear in the general description of the nongraded program, it is essential that no child be placed in any one type of group and allowed to remain there

PUPIL'S EVALUATION SHEET FOR PLACEMENT

Name _____ Date _____

_____ AGE (May)

_____ IQ (latest)

_____ ACHIEVEMENT TEST SCORE (reading)

_____ READING MAGAZINE TEST SCORE

_____ GRADE CARD EVALUATION (reading)

_____ CHECK APPROPRIATE BOX OF LAST READING LEVEL AND MAGAZINE

1	2	3	4	5	6	7	8	9
☐	☐	☐	☐	☐	☐	☐	☐	☐

9a	10	11	12	13	14	15	15a
☐	☐	☐	☐	☐	☐	☐	☐

Pupil has completed: Book and Page _____

LEARNING ABILITY

Rapid	Fast	Ave.	Slow	V. Slow
☐	☐	☐	☐	☐

TEACHER COMMENTS AND RECOMMENDATION

_____

Please list any unusual characteristics of the pupil's which his next teacher should know. Physical handicaps - hearing - speaking - vision - the arts - talents - interests - needs - or any other:

_____

_____

_____

indefinitely. Flexibility should be the keynote for grouping. In general, the types of grouping provisions discussed below are those which should be employed.

Achievement Grouping

Observers of nongraded programs have come to the conclusion that grouping of students according to levels of achievement in the skill subjects for a portion of the school day is desirable and should be done at the elementary school level. The achievement grouping patterns should be flexible, however, so that children can move from level to level during the skill development period. Achievement grouping enables the teacher to narrow the range of achievement among children in the skill subjects. Some provisions for achievement grouping for a portion of the day should be made in any elementary school developing or conducting a nongraded program.

The chart below illustrates one group of children grouped by achievement for language arts in the Transition Division, ages 7-9, in the Benton Elementary School, St. Charles, Missouri. Children were grouped and regrouped in this achievement range according to needs.

BENTON CONTINUOUS PROGRESS SCHOOL
St. Charles, Missouri
HOMOGENEOUS GROUPING FOR LANGUAGE ARTS
TRANSITION DIVISION — Ages 7-9

Child	Rating	Year in School
1.	3.1	4
2.	3.1	3
3.	3.1	3
4.	3.0	4
5.	3.0	3
6.	3.0	3
7.	3.0	4
8.	3.0	4
9.	3.0	3
10.	3.0	5
11.	2.9	3
12.	2.9	4
13.	2.9	4
14.	2.9	4
15.	2.9	4

16.	2.8	4
17.	2.8	4
18.	2.7	4
19.	2.6	4
20.	2.5	4
21.	2.5	3
22.	2.5	4
23.	2.4	3
24.	2.3	4
25.	2.0	3
26.	2.0	3

After much study of past records, observation of teachers, and present test data, children in the Skill Division, ages 6 and 7 at Benton Elementary School, St. Charles, Missouri, were grouped according to the following procedures in homogeneous grouping situations for language arts:

1. The first year children who attended kindergarten were grouped according to the results of the Metropolitan Readiness Test.

2. First year children who had no kindergarten experience were listed alphabetically in one group and were regrouped as soon as the necessary information was available for proper placement for instructional purposes.

3. The second year children were grouped according to the results of the Stanford Achievement tests.

4. Teacher judgment regarding placement of second year children took into consideration the age, physical maturity, siblings, work habits, social attitudes, and previous teacher-pupil-relationship.

Acceleration

The nongraded school should provide for acceleration. This specialized form of grouping can help reduce the range of variability within the classroom and at the same time lessen the boredom and dissatisfaction of bright students. Educators should not ignore the compelling logic and impressive evidence that can be compiled in favor of moderate acceleration. In the nongraded program, provision should be made for early admission to kindergarten and the first year of school and for accelerated progression to the junior high level for

GROUPING

the very bright youngsters who are socially and emotionally capable of the acceleration.

Acceleration alone, as with grouping of any kind, in the nongraded elementary school does not constitute an adequate program for bright children. Acceleration is primarily an administrative procedure and should be a part of every program for gifted children, but it does not obviate the necessity for other modifications of the standard school routine, especially in the area of curriculum content and organization.

As stated before, some children can progress through a prescribed amount of material at a much faster rate. The organizational pattern below illustrates nongraded language arts levels used for grouping purposes in most schools. Children progress from level to level at their own rate of progress; they move from level to level or from room to room during this period if necessary. In this type of organization, language arts is the only nongraded portion of the program, and achievement grouping is used as a technique for placing the children in instructional levels. *We cannot overstress the idea that grouping by levels should not be rigid.*

I. NONGRADED LANGUAGE ARTS IN RELATION TO THE TOTAL PROGRAM
   Abingdon Elementary School, Abingdon, Virginia

Level			
	1	Readiness	Children are grouped in reading as a basis for the language arts program. Children progress from level to level at their own rate of progress, and move from room to room during this period if necessary.
	2	Pre-Primer	
	3	Primer	
	4	First	
	5	Second[1]	
	6	Second[2]	
	7	Third[1]	
	8	Third[2]	The language arts, with reading as a basis for grouping, should also include listening, speaking, and writing experiences.
	9	Fourth	
	10	Fifth	
	11	Sixth	
	12	Enrichment	

Mathematics—Children are grouped according to needs, ability, and achievement in the self-contained classroom. The children move from their self-contained classroom to another room if necessary.

Unit Teaching
Social Studies
Science and Health   (Art and Music correlated)

Time is allotted for skill development in art and music.
Physical Education is scheduled in the program throughout the day.

Heterogeneous Grouping

In establishing grouping variations for the nongraded school, educators should plan for children to spend 40 to 50 percent of their time with other children differing in socio-economic status, cultural background, range of abilities, special talents and interests, and personal needs. When grouping children heterogeneously, educators should group and regroup children in large groups and small groups in order that they may share interests, talents, and leadership abilities and learn how to work, play, and plan together.

The chart on page 65 depicts sixty children working in a heterogeneous nongraded team teaching grouping situation in large group, small groups, and individually.

The children at Benton Elementary School, St. Charles, Missouri, were grouped in the content areas in heterogeneous grouping situations. The following procedures were followed to group the children in the Skills Division, ages 6 and 7 in flexible group situations:

1. First year children who had not attended kindergarten or who rate "poor risk" on the Metropolitan Readiness Tests were arranged alphabetically in two groups, girls and boys.

2. First year children who had attended kindergarten were grouped according to the results of the Metropolitan Readiness Tests as "average" and "above average," then arranged alphabetically in two groups, boys and girls.

3. Second year children were divided into two groups, boys and girls, then arranged from "high" to "low" according to scores on the Stanford Achievement Tests.

GROUPING

4. The children were placed with the six teachers of the Skills Division by repeating a one through six distribution until all the children were placed.

5. We began with the "high" girl on the list of second year children and followed through to the "low" girl, then used the same procedure for second year boys.

6. Next, the first year children beginning with the first girl on the "above average" list and following through to the last boy on the "average" list were placed.

7. Children having no kindergarten training were placed from the alphabetical list of girls and boys.

8. Consideration was given so that no second year child was placed with a homeroom teacher who had been his or her first year teacher.

9. Some adjustment was made when one teacher had a much larger number of boys than girls.
   Thus the children of the Skills Division were divided into six heterogeneous groups.

x x x x x x x x x x x x x x x x x x x x x x x x x x x x x x x x x x x x x x x x x x x x x x x x x x x x x x x x x x x x	Grouped together by age in large group situations

x x x   x x x
x x x   x x x
x x x   x x x
x x x   x x x
     x
     x
x x   x
x x
	Regrouped by interest, talents, and achievement in small groups and individually

x x
   x   x x   x
x x   x x   x x
x x   x x   x x x
x
   x x x x x x x x x	

CONTENT AREA ORGANIZATION
SOCIAL STUDIES—SCIENCE—HEALTH
P.E.—ART—MUSIC

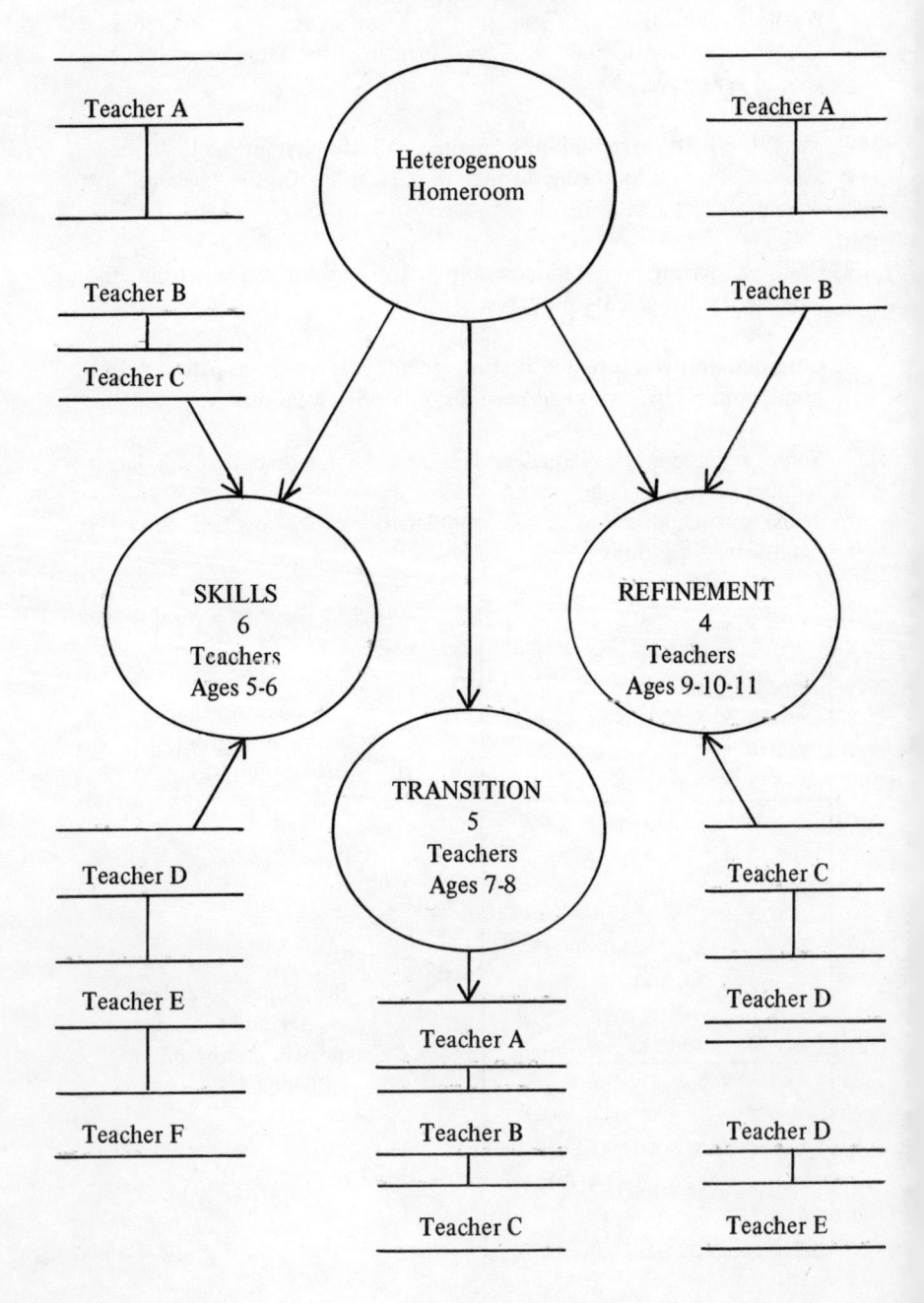

Teacher A

Teacher B

Teacher C

Heterogenous Homeroom

Teacher A

Teacher B

SKILLS
6
Teachers
Ages 5-6

REFINEMENT
4
Teachers
Ages 9-10-11

Teacher D

Teacher E

Teacher F

TRANSITION
5
Teachers
Ages 7-8

Teacher C

Teacher D

Teacher A

Teacher B

Teacher C

Teacher D

Teacher E

The chart on page 66 depicts the heterogenous grouping arrangements of Benton Elementary School, St. Charles, Missouri.

NONGRADED—TEAM TEACHING APPROACH, STRESSING INDIVIDUALIZATION

At Tusculum View Elementary School, Greenville, Tennessee, the faculty organized into teams, a primary team and an intermediate team. The key to the program was success—that is, finding the place where each individual pupil may experience some type of success daily in all areas of the curriculum. The organization was a nongraded one with neither grades (first, second, third, etc.) nor levels (I, II, III, IV) used in the organizational structure. Children worked at their own rate, and progressed at their own rate of growth. The chart on page 68 illustrates their organizational pattern.

The Dyersburg Elementary School, Dyersburg, Tennessee, also used a team teaching approach in a nongraded skills program with sixty-nine students, two teachers, one aide, a librarian, a music teacher, a physical education teacher, and the principal were utilized on the team. As illustrated on page 69, the mathematics and reading programs were nongraded making no group more than twenty-four when the teachers teamed with the librarian and the principal. These small groups permitted teachers to individualize the skill subjects. The physical education and music teacher, with the help of the aide, took sixty-nine children in a large group situation giving the team of reading and mathematics teachers time to plan at least twice a week.

Individualization of Instruction

Provision for the independent study form of grouping in the nongraded school permits each child to select topics of particular interest and pursue them in depth. It also makes possible effective use of such individualized material and media as programmed materials, teaching machines, and education kits which allow children to progress at their own personal rates of development. Those developing nongraded programs should provide time for personalized study and thus capitalize on the individual child's ability and motivation to learn without direct and constant teacher supervision. Teachers should be trained to act as learning consultants or resource persons in this type of situation.

Another type of nongraded grouping within a graded situation

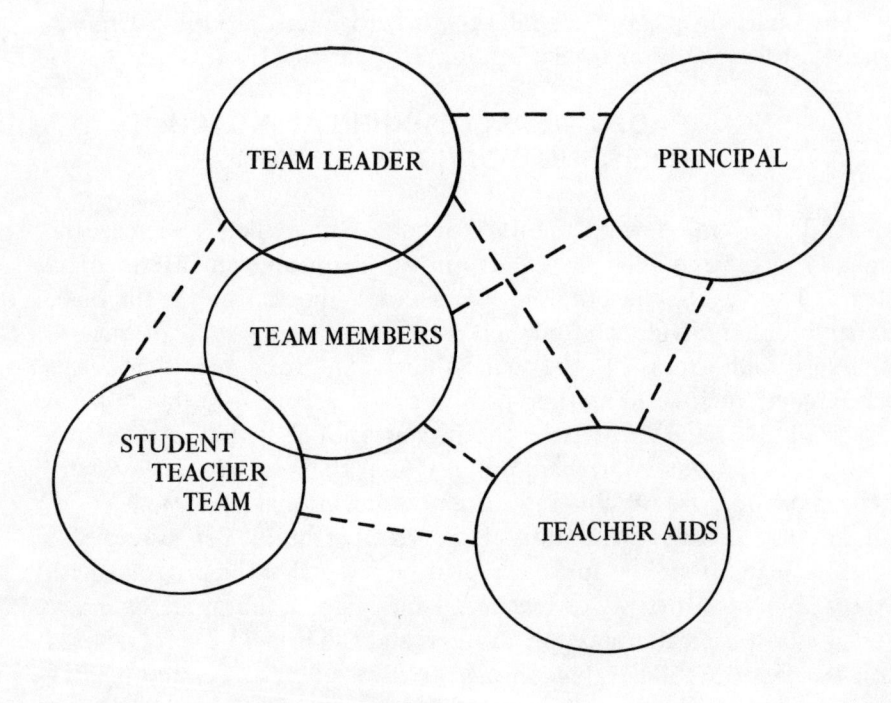

```
        ┌─────────────┐         ┌─────────────┐
        │ TEAM LEADER │         │  PRINCIPAL  │
        └─────────────┘         └─────────────┘
        ┌─────────────┐
        │ TEAM MEMBERS│
        └─────────────┘
    ┌─────────┐
    │ STUDENT │
    │ TEACHER │            ┌─────────────┐
    │  TEAM   │            │ TEACHER AIDS│
    └─────────┘            └─────────────┘
```

which attempts to individualize instruction may revolutionize educators in the years ahead. It is called individually prescribed instruction. It allows the child to learn mathematics, reading, science, and spelling at his own individual pace.

In this nongraded program, the children use a learning center—a large room with inexpensive, but sturdy record players and their attached earphones placed along the walls. They also use adjoining rooms for individual work. Teachers and the school librarian act as coordinators and tutors as the pupils proceeded with the various materials.

Most of the pupils work independently. Some listen to the record players and complete workbooks as directed by the recording voice. Some repeat sounds as directed by the record. Others work with programmed printed material at tables in the adjoining rooms. A few get materials for their "next step" from carefully numbered files located in the middle of the learning center. The teacher gives the children aid when it is needed. Teacher aides correct the tests before the child forgets what he did wrong.

SCHEDULE FOR TEAM TEACHING IN A NONGRADED SITUATION

(Fifth year children)

	8:45-9:15	9:35-10:25	10:40-11:30	11:30-12:10	1:00-2:00	2:30-3:15
	Reading and Library	Reading and Library	Math	English	Health-Science Music	P.E.
Library	32	37				
Hime	19	17	24	35	35	
Sudbury	18	15	21	34	34	
Daniels			24			
Rone Music-Thurs.					1:20-2:05	
Dodds						

GROUPING AND REGROUPING IN A FLEXIBLE SCHEDULE ORGANIZATIONAL PLAN CONTINUOUS PROGRESS SCHOOL

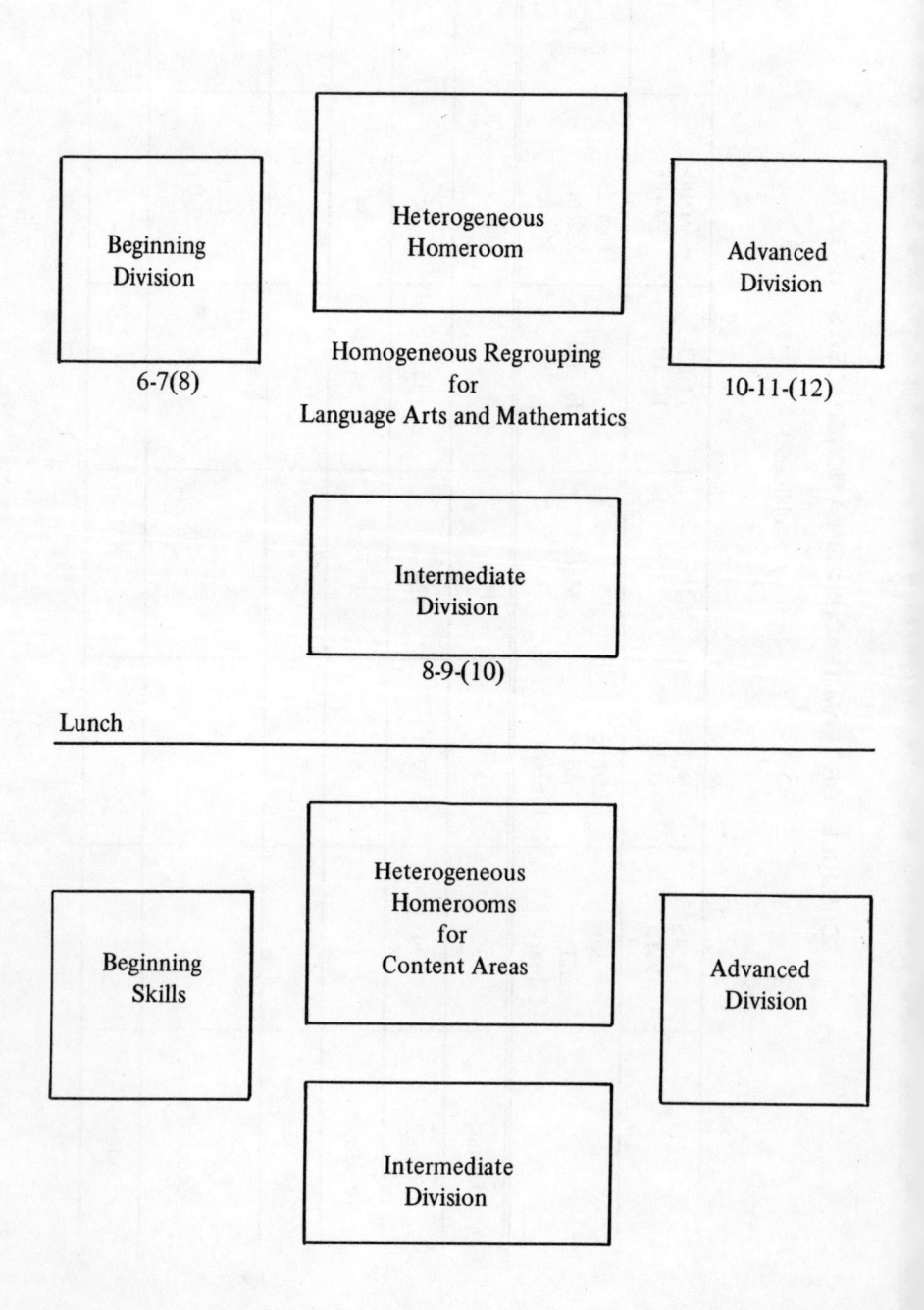

Beginning Division

6-7(8)

Heterogeneous Homeroom

Homogeneous Regrouping for
Language Arts and Mathematics

Advanced Division

10-11-(12)

Intermediate Division

8-9-(10)

Lunch

Beginning Skills

Heterogeneous Homerooms for Content Areas

Advanced Division

Intermediate Division

GROUPING AND REGROUPING IN A FLEXIBLE SCHEDULE

As stated before, children do not remain in any given group all day. The next chart depicts a nongraded organization. Children are grouped by age in heterogeneous clusters in homeroom; from there they are grouped and regrouped homogeneously for skill development in language arts and mathematics. They are allowed to progress at their own rate from level to level within the division and/or divisions.

The children return to their heterogeneous homeroom for content area subjects. Here they are grouped and regrouped by achievement, interest, and talents. In these content areas, the skill division groups are closely supervised; the transition division groups are given much more independent work; and a great amount of the child's time in the refinement division is devoted to independent study.

Since few children should remain in any one grouping situation the whole day, the nongraded plan groups children by ability and age in the skill development periods. Here children are grouped and regrouped during these skill development periods; they are allowed to progress at their own rate.

They are regrouped in heterogeneous grouping arrangements in the content areas. Here, too, children progress through a progression of learning experiences which stress creativity and problem solving. Small group discussions and individual work is encouraged in these heterogeneous groups.

Pretests, skill sheets, daily performance, and post tests help the teacher determine when a child is ready for another phase or level of development in the program. Evaluation is continuous in order to keep the grouping arrangements flexible.

The organizational chart presented on page 70 clearly illustrates grouping and regrouping in a flexible school situation.

SUMMARY

As previously suggested, criteria express intent but do not suggest the cut-off points characteristic of standards. However, in some instances of grouping it may be that staff decisions run toward the setting of standards or the establishment of definite cut-off points to determine inclusions in or exclusion from specific groups. If and when and to the extent that any staff decides upon the use of standards, they should be specifically stated, written down, and thoroughly understood by all involved in their use. However, in most instances more flexible bases of judgment will be more helpful and less likely to do injustice to the pupils grouped. Most nongraded schools are moving toward pupil-teacher standards; they are fitting, as much as possible, the material around the needs of the child.

It will be noted that it is essential to ask many questions about any suggested grouping to determine its feasibility. The criteria suggested should rather thoroughly indicate all of the kinds of decisions that are necessary to assure that groups, once formed, have a chance to fulfill some majority of the school purposes. However, very few groups will ever fulfill them all; e.g., draw a thoughtful and positive response to the questions asked.

As illustrated by the grouping patterns in this chapter, achievement grouping tends to narrow the range of abilities in a group; acceleration allows for the gifted child to progress at a faster rate; heterogeneous grouping places different types of children together for social purposes; and individualized instruction or independent study permits the child to progress at an individual pace and to pursue his own interests in depth.

As stated before in the chapter, good grouping involves many factors, is always temporary, and should be considered subject to any change or adjustment which experience shows to be desirable in the accomplishment of school purposes. *Needs are never group needs; they are always individual needs,* sometimes common to the several members of the group. Therefore, if the approximate individualization of instruction is a serious purpose of a nongraded school program, an appropriate type of grouping is nearly always necessary to accomplish it. It must be understood that no child should stay in any one grouping situation all day; flexibility is the keynote.

The differences of teachers, specialists, and aides should be considered as well as the differences of children.

4

Team Teaching Within the Nongraded Structure

ADVANTAGES OF THE TEAM APPROACH

Although there are many variations in teams, all team teaching is based on the premise that teachers can accomplish more when they combine their talents while working together than working alone. Team teaching has been defined by several authorities as any form of teaching in which two or more teachers meet regularly and plan purposefully shared responsibility for a group of children. This shared responsibility encompasses long and short range planning, large group, small group and individual presentations, and cooperative evaluation for two or more classes of children.

The key words in team teaching are "team planning." Too many elementary schools engage in "so-called" team teaching when it is no more than "teacher-exchanging," recognizing of course the special talents of the teachers.

Team teaching is an organizational pattern, within which the school can greatly improve the quality of its instructional program.

Team teaching goes hand-in-hand with curriculum improvement through:

(1) provision for large group, small group, and independent study;

(2) better use of the complete staff and resource persons;

(3) greater flexibility in space and equipment;

(4) more cooperative planning, and

(5) increased use of audio-visual aids and technology.

Some of the assumptions which seem to underscore current proposals for school practice and staff utilization are:

1. Members of the faculty do not function as well in isolation from the staff.

2. Teachers have special talents that should be shared.

3. Effective curriculum planning requires teacher responsibility for implementation.

4. Relationships among the different fields of content should be developed.

5. Schools should be flexible enough that students may move ahead in their studies according to their abilities.

6. Schools should supplement their programs with the talents of citizens.

7. Team leaders should be given extra pay and recognition for their leadership.

8. Teachers have a responsibility for assisting in the training of new teachers and auxiliary personnel.

9. There is more regard for learning and scholarship.

10. Children get to know other children in other classes.

Some of the advantages of team teaching discussed by Dr. Lynn Canady in the Appalachian Advance are:

TEAM TEACHING

1. Team teaching can encourage versatility and originality of presentations with several teachers planning and working together and sharing the tasks.

2. There is evidence that team teaching makes possible a more flexible grouping of children than the traditional self-contained classrooms.

3. Students will benefit from various teachers' viewpoints and methods of teaching.

4. Team teaching makes it possible to capitalize on teacher assets and individual differences of teachers.

5. Supporters of team teaching argue that the process encourages better evaluation since several teachers are asked to give their individual judgments as to the effectiveness of teaching methods as well as pupil achievement and growth.

6. Independent study, a part of team teaching, helps the child become excited about and responsible for his learning.

7. It enables the teacher to meet both the emotional needs and content interests of children.

8. It offers an excellent method for teachers to obtain professional growth among teachers.

9. Intern teachers and auxiliary personnel have an opportunity to plan and work with more than one teacher.[1]

DISADVANTAGES OF THE TEAM APPROACH

Some of the disadvantages of team teaching are:

1. Some teachers find it difficult to work together in a team teaching situation.

2. A few children find it difficult to adjust to more than one teacher.

3. Some teachers feel that it is difficult to keep a continuity in the learning experience of children when more than one teacher is involved in the teaching and evaluation.

---
[1] Lynn R. Canady, "Team Teaching: Is It for Me?" *Appalachian Advance.* Vol. S. No. 5, (Feb., 1969) pp. 10-17.

4. Finding space for large group, small group and individual instruction is difficult in some schools.

5. Time for cooperative planning must be provided during the day and many administrators cannot provide all teachers of the team with the same free period of time.

ASPECTS OF TEAM TEACHING PLANS

Team teaching demands increased expertise from its teachers, interns, and auxiliary personnel. Since it is organized to capitalize on individual talents for instruction and curriculum study it is essential that the total team members operate at increasingly higher levels of performance.

Much of the leadership on a team is shared, therefore, there must be a cooperative approach to teaming. Leadership is essential for effective coordination of the total team unit. The team leader has little authority, therefore, leadership in this role is challenging. Since the team demands that there be a variety of instructional methods used, teachers need extensive in-service training. The team members need workable techniques for large and small group instruction; for plans organizing and supervising independent study; and knowledge in using computers, audio-visuals, programmed material and specialized equipment.

The principal must coordinate the teams' efforts. Most principals work through the team leaders. This role requires the principal to have a greater knowledge of his staff, the children, and the curriculum. In their roles the team leader and team free him from many details.

Since children learn from teachers, from each other, and independently, the team must find basic ways to plan lessons in each grouping situation. They develop objectives, determine curriculum content, and plan essential concepts to be taught.

The team must find an appropriate way to introduce their plan through large groups, small groups, and individual instruction.

The Tusculum View Elementary team teaching chart on page 77 illustrates the structure of their team teaching plan; it also shows the roles of personnel involved in a nongraded situation. As this chart illustrates, the team must be organized in order that each person knows his responsibility on the team. As stated before, team teaching is an organizational pattern that enables the school to improve the

TEAM TEACHING

TUSCULUM VIEW ELEMENTARY ORGANIZATIONAL CHART

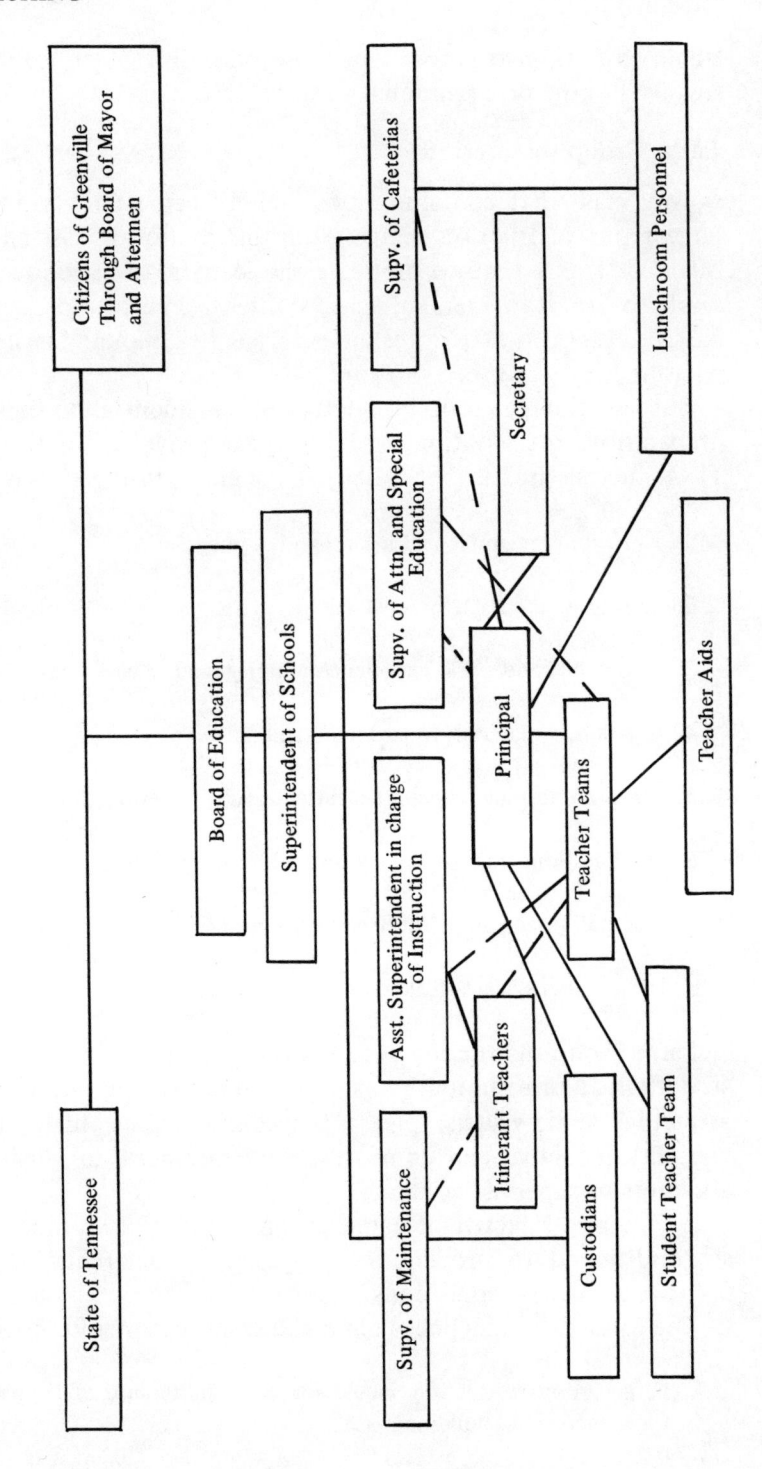

- Citizens of Greenville Through Board of Mayor and Aldermen
- State of Tennessee
- Board of Education
- Superintendent of Schools
- Supv. of Cafeterias
- Supv. of Attn. and Special Education
- Asst. Superintendent in charge of Instruction
- Supv. of Maintenance
- Secretary
- Principal
- Itinerant Teachers
- Lunchroom Personnel
- Teacher Teams
- Teacher Aids
- Custodians
- Student Teacher Team

quality of its instruction. To accomplish this objective all who are involved in the program must cooperate.

Large Group Instruction

Any class that contains more than fifteen students provides for large group instruction. Large group instruction is basically teacher-directed. It is a time to motivate the learner, to introduce a unit of work, or to learn general basic content. The learner is physically passive except to take notes; he is very active mentally as he reacts to what he learns and sees.

Successful large group instruction is dependent upon these factors: preparation, presentation, and the space provided for the audience. These factors are also essential if large group instruction is effective:

1. Keep content simple and meaningful as possible.

2. Use clever and colorful illustrations.

3. Know the child's past experiences, interest and achievement.

4. Relate new materials to past experiences.

5. Stress interest and conceptualization against memorization.

6. Use questions that might be answered by the group as a whole.

7. Use multi-media in presenting many large group presentations.

8. Use a sound system so children can be heard.

Large group instruction requires thorough preparation and careful study. Great care should be exercised in presenting the content, e.g., attractive audio-visuals, pleasant speaking voices, high interest in content, attractive and comfortable environment, and instructional assistants to supervise students.

It is more effective if large group instruction rooms could be air-conditioned to provide for proper air and circulation. Carpets improve acoustical conditions.

The following guidelines help make team teaching functional:

1. Large group instruction should make for better use of the teacher's time, energy and building space.

TEAM TEACHING 79

2. Large group instruction should range from twenty minutes to forty minutes in the elementary school. The length of the period depends upon (1) the effectiveness of the teacher; (2) the interest in the subject and; (3) the climate of the room.

3. The frequency of large-group instruction should be flexible. This depends upon the needs of the children, adequate large group space and the experience of the teachers in large group situations.

4. Large group instruction should be effective in any elementary subject. It is not the subject; it is the manner in which it is presented.

5. One should always use the best audio-visuals available when presenting large group instruction.

6. All teachers should prepare the students for listening skills to be used in large group situations.

Small Groups at Work

In small groups children can discuss problems, communicate effectively, respect the opinions of others, and think together with children of diverse backgrounds.

Small group discussions encourage children to cut across content lines, project into the future, grasp content in depth, generalize after much research, and do critical and analytical thinking. Teachers and students do not worry if the groups are not covering predetermined content. Teachers become resource persons and/or co-participants with the group. Students also take part in being observers, recorders, and leaders.

The following suggestions serve as guidelines for educators planning small group discussions:

1. Groups should be made flexible in order that children may have an opportunity to work and discuss with different kinds of children. Such facts as age, friendships, maturity, sex, interests, and goals of the children help determine the grouping and regrouping of children in the seminars.

2. Groups should never be more than fifteen children and it might be desirable for the children in the elementary school to meet for approximately twenty to thirty minutes.

The following chart illustrates types of activities appropriate for large and small group instruction.

SUGGESTED LARGE AND SMALL GROUPS INSTRUCTIONAL ACTIVITIES

SUBJECT	LARGE	SMALL
Reading	Dramatization Choral Speaking Testing Vocabulary Film on the Story Presented	Oral reading Listening center (phonics, dictionary, etc.) Supervised related activities Remedial instruction Building vocabulary Testing Phonics Viewing center
Spelling	Vocabulary Written practice Sentence dictation Word meaning Testing	Extension of vocabulary for able Reduction of vocabulary for slow Analysis of words Dictionary study
Handwriting	Introduction of letter form Improvement of common errors Practice Filmstrip on writing	Special help

TEAM TEACHING

SUGGESTED LARGE AND SMALL GROUPS INSTRUCTIONAL ACTIVITIES *(continued)*

SUBJECT	LARGE	SMALL
Language	Introduction of new skills Presentation of oral reports Reinforcements of skills Testing	Special help Creative writing Preparation of oral reports Testing
Mathematics	Film on new meanings Introduction of new skills Clarification of concepts Testing	Extension of skills for able Simplification of terms for slow Remedial instruction Testing
Science	Introduce Science words Introduction of new units Concluding activity of unit Demonstration of experiment Testing	Individual experiments Reinforcement of basic skills Testing Creative writing Simplification of material
Social Studies	Introduction of new units Clarification of concepts Concluding activities of unit Field trips Resource persons	Study skills - maps - etc. Committee activities Simplification of material Creative activities Construction

3. The objective of small group discussion should be to develop attitudes, values, and social skills.

4. Special training should be given the elementary children in how to work in small groups, e.g., duties of the leader, recorder and observer, deciding on issues to be discussed, planning of operation, and summarizing the discussions.

5. The team leader, consultants, or aides must observe the behavior of the group in order to help them as individuals and as a group member.

Independent Study

During the independent study period children should be allowed to study in depth on a subject of their own interest. Topics for selection should also be listed in the form of problem areas.

Children need an opportunity to study and work away from the mass. Here they can develop responsibility for their own learning, each according to his own interest and rate of ability. Independent study also gives the child an opportunity to pursue a problem in depth, to be as creative as he wishes, and to explore various fields of interest.

No other method of grouping permits different rates of progress by students as much as independent study. The independent study approach allows the day to be flexible for the child. He moves to another phase of his study when he is ready to move.

During the independent study, the child "learns to learn" on his own. The child must learn to use the research tools in order to be an effective independent learner. While working "on his own" he selects, uses, and evaluates many kinds of media to find answers for his problems.

Following are suggestions educators should follow when introducing independent study:

1. Students placed in independent studies must possess self-reliance and be taught the skill to work independently.

2. The students with limited abilities shall have small assignments and more supervision.

3. Students working in independent studies should know how to evaluate their progress.

TEAM TEACHING

4. The basis for placing children in independent study are: (a) ability to work independently, (b) interest in the subject, and (c) the progress the child is making.

5. Independent subject instruction requires a variety of materials e.g., films, records, filmstrips, reference books, texts, pictures, models, computers, listening centers, magazines, teaching machines, and programmed materials. Work rooms for the children need to be provided with flexible carrels, flexible furniture and appropriate laboratories to enable the children to work effectively.

The topics below are examples of depth study projects as used in a "Pacific Coast Region Unit" in the intermediate years at Barger Elementary School in Chattanooga, Tennessee.

Choose one or more of the following topics and prepare a tape, paper, talk, skit, panel discussion or model (where appropriate) to show you have a thorough knowledge of the topic. You may decide to work in small groups on some of the projects.

1. Tournament of Roses and the Rose Bowl Game
2. Disneyland
3. The California Movie Industry (Hollywood)
4. The Gold Rush of 1849
5. Stagecoaches of the West
6. Covered Wagons (models)
7. A Spanish Mission (models)
8. Seasonal Changes of the Sierras
9. The Redwood Giants or The Redwood Highway
10. Tales of Paul Bunyan
11. San Francisco's Fisherman's Wharf
12. Chinatown, U.S.A.
13. The Golden Gate Bridge (models)
14. The 1962 Seattle World's Fair
15. Gold Dredging (models), Panning for Gold
16. Eskimo Homes (models)
17. The San Francisco Cable Cars
18. The Redwood Highway
19. Alcan Highway
20. Knott's Berry Farm

21. Totem Poles (models made from soap)
22. Salmon Fishing
23. Various National Parks of the Pacific Coast region
24. Clothes Worn by the Various People of the Pacific Coast Region (models)
25. Various Modes of Transportation of the Pacific Coast Region (models)
26. Alcatraz

STAFF PLANNING

Staff planning is essential for effective team teaching programs. It is imperative that the staff plan cooperatively with the regular team as well as with the auxiliary personnel, specialists, and resource persons.

In most of the team-staff planning teams, the members work together to develop plans for instruction, they determine together the best ways in which their individual teaching competencies can be used in the realization of their plans, and they jointly evaluate the progress made by their pupils.

The following are functional guidelines for staff planning and implementation.

GUIDELINES FOR TEAM FUNCTIONING

I. Role Differentiation of Members

   A. Specific competencies or deficiencies of team members are taken into consideration when the instructional program is planned.

   B. Team members may assume completely different roles.

   1. Teachers may be utilized as academic advisors, subject matter resource persons, etc.

   2. A teacher may devote time fully to planning or preparing materials for team members.

   C. A hierarchial arrangement with a team leader and an assistant leader is appropriate in some instances.

TEAM TEACHING

II. Decision Making

   A. The team determines its own organization in cooperation with the principal.

   1. The team may assign members various responsibilities such as meeting chairman, team communicator, etc.

   2. A team leader is necessary to improve team functioning.

   3. All team teachers have an opportunity to participate in decision making with the team leader.

   4. The team determines meeting times and agenda.

III. Flexibility in Instructional Groups

   A. Team teaching permits the use of large and small instructional groups as well as independent study designed to implement specific activities.

   B. Team teaching makes it possible to regroup frequently to achieve a greater homogeneity when desirable for teaching skills.

   1. Periodic regrouping in some skills areas is necessary to provide a better way of meeting individual needs.

   2. Group stability can be developed by retaining fairly constant groups in areas such as social studies, music and physical education.

   3. Social groups which include interage grouping give children of similar and varied maturational levels an opportunity to interact.

   4. Regrouping encourages special interest, talent and hobby groups.

IV. Use of Certified Resource Persons and Non-certified Personnel

   A. Certified resource persons often allow for greater specialization in certain areas and add to the resources available to the classroom teacher.

1. The use of part-time personnel may add to the flexibility of the program.

2. The resource person may serve to reduce the pupil-teacher ratio at any given time.

B. Non-certificated personnel and teacher aides may be employed to relieve the teacher of many routine duties and tasks.

1. Three specialized aides may be acquired in the place of one staff member.

2. Teachers need to explore the many ways in which aides can be effectively used in the classroom.

V. Social Climate of the Learning Environment

A. Social interaction among pupils and with elements of the environment is fostered.

B. Pupils are delegated more freedom and therefore learn to assume more responsibility for their own behavior and learning.

C. A relaxed self-disciplined atmosphere prevails and the structure of the environment tends to be very fluid, fostering individual growth according to unique rates in learning.

D. The individual is the center of the learning environment and may initiate many of his own activities as well as participating in teacher directed groups.

VI. Evaluation of Individual and Team Effectiveness

A. Team members should evaluate their effectiveness on both the planning level and the operational level.

B. Team members may cooperatively share new ideas and new approaches to old problems.

C. Each team member may have the opportunity to identify problem areas within the existing instructional program and make suggestions for improvement.

1. Each member should assume the responsibility of adding pertinent data when needed.

2. The team should evaluate its effectiveness in making a decision related to a problem and then implementing this decision.

D. Teachers working together may evaluate teaching techniques.

1. Compatibility among team personnel is important.

2. Feedback related to teaching techniques is valuable when rapport between teachers is established.

E. The team can better evaluate pupils when observing them from many points of view.

LONG AND SHORT RANGE PLANS

In our judgment the concept of planning must consist of long range and short range plans. The team "leader," curriculum director, principal, team members, aides, and specialists must develop long and short range plans. It is the only feasible way to insure that the new curricula being developed will be understood and executed well enough to be accepted by teachers and made worthwhile for pupils.

The long and short range plans also help to insure that each child will have at least one teacher with whom he relates well and who may in time be able to assist other team members in their approach to the child.

The sample long range plan which follows places fifth year children in large and small groups for a broad Language Arts and Social Studies unit, prepared under the supervision of Mrs. Amendia Carroll Cate and Dr. Lynn Canady who were supervisors of the Chattanooga Team Teaching Project and the principal of Barger Elementary School, Mrs. Ruth McCafferty.

"LONG RANGE PLANS FOR CONTENT AREA"

FIFTH YEAR TEAM—BARGER ELEMENTARY SCHOOL, CHATTANOOGA, TENNESSEE
"THE PACIFIC COAST REGION"

A Language Arts and Social Studies Unit

Each teacher should check where his or her name appears. Do you know and understand what your responsibilities are? Where to go? What to do? We must work on a plan for informing the students of their various group assignments with as little confusion for them and teachers as possible. (LGI—large group instruction, combining all groups; LG—large group, and SG—small group).

Monday, February 27

12:30 — 1:00 LGI   Introduction of Unit   CANADY

California: An Overview   SMITH

1:00 — 1:30   Approximately one-half of the fifth grade students (45) will be grouped into three small groups for follow-up or supplementary instruction to the LGI. Each of the small groups should contain not more than 15 students. SG I should report with MRS. PETERS to her regular classroom. SG II should report to the Resource Center with MRS. COOK. SG III should report with MR. SMITH to his end of the large room. The remaining 45 students should assemble in Mrs. Cook's end of the large room with DR. CANADY to receive information pertaining to vocabulary, spelling, independent study projects and a bibliography related to the unit.

The SG's should review the materials presented in LGI, the essential facts which Mr. Smith has given to the other teachers on the team, rules and techniques of small group discussion, and, if time permits, attempt to develop some interest or curiosity in the concepts included in the unit and distributed to the teachers by MR. SMITH.

1:30 — 2:00   Reverse the groups and repeat the activities described above.

TEAM TEACHING

	If possible, between 1:00 and 2:00 P.M., MRS. SHAW and at least one of the instructional aides should help the teacher (MRS. COOK) in the Resource Center with the students using the listening stations filmstrip previewers, and other materials.
2:00 – 2:15 LGI	All students go to the Cafetorium where MRS. SHAW will introduce the song: "California, Here I Come."

Tuesday, February 28

12:30 – 1:00 LGI	16 mm film: "California: A View of the Golden State"
	MR. SMITH to be in charge.
	Emphasis on the skill of reading charts and graphs (using data from the unit) MR. SMITH
	Introduction of art activity—SMITH
1:00 – 1:35 SGs LG	Students should assemble as they did on Monday except MRS. SHAW should meet with MR. SMITH's group, and they probably will have to meet on the stage. Students in the small groups will work on an art activity as introduced in LGI by MR. SMITH.
	The remaining 45 students should assemble in MR. SMITH's end of the large room to be shown slides of California, Disneyland, etc., and to receive a homework assignment on descriptive writing.
1:30 – 2:10 SGs LG	Reverse groups and repeat activities.

Wednesday, March 1

12:30 – 1:00 LGI	Introduction to the states of Washington and Oregon. MR. SMITH.
1:00 – 1:30 SGs	All students assemble into small groups of approximately 15 each to share their descriptive writing homework assignments and to select one assignment to be shared with the LG. Teachers to meet with the five groups are: SMITH, PETERS, COOK, SHAW, CANADY, SULLIVAN or McCAFFERTY.

Meeting places include: 3 regular classrooms, Resource Center, Library or stage (to be determined).

1:30 – 2:15   45 students meet in auditorium for music activities related to the unit.

45 students meet in library and Resource Center to work on independent projects, bibliography readings, listening station activities, previewing filmstrips, etc. MR. SMITH and at least ONE INSTRUCTIONAL AIDE will be responsible for the other 45. MRS. COOK and MRS. PETERS can be planning for other activities of the unit.

12:30 – 1:00 LGI   16 mm film: "The Salmon Story" MR. SMITH. Review of essential facts pertaining to Oregon and the state of Washington. (SMITH)

1:00 – 1:30 SG   Students assemble into regular homeroom groups for instruction in the vocabulary and spelling words of the unit. (SMITH, COOK, PETERS)

1:30 – 2:15   Repeat the activities scheduled for this block of time on Wednesday, March 1, except the groups are reversed.

Friday, March 3
12:30 – 1:15 SG   Students assemble into regular homeroom groups with their teachers (SMITH, PETERS, COOK) and review the material of the unit in preparation for their quiz, determine and assist progress on independent projects. In fact, some students can be excused from this session if the individual teachers feel the student or students can profit more from working on individual projects or from examining materials in the Resource Center (AIDE)– review filmstrips, slides, tapes, records, etc.

1:15 – 2:00 LGI   Quiz (CANADY, if available, SMITH and COOK)

After instructions are given about the quiz, MRS. COOK may take the students in her reading class to the Resource Center to take the test. Those students may use the listening stations and have the test questions read to them. If teachers do not feel any students will need the questions read to them, both MRS. COOK and MRS. PETERS may use this time for planning additional unit activities.

TEAM TEACHING

2:00 – 2:15 LGI   All students sing the songs introduced during the unit with MRS. SHAW in charge. Meet in the cafeteria.

NOTES: Please plan ahead. If there are conflicts with time, space or persons, let's resolve them when we meet after school Monday, February 27. Keep in mind that the numbers in groups should be determined by what you plan to do and considering the various needs of the individuals in the groups.

The outline below illustrates long range content plans by a team consisting of three teachers, special teachers in art and music, an aide, a librarian, and ninety-five children.

"LONG RANGE PLANNING—TEAM TEACHING"

RESOURCE UNIT

TITLE: LEARNING TO LIVE WITH OUR NEIGHBORS (MEXICO)

TEAM MEMBERS: 3 Teachers   Special Teachers
               Librarian   Aide

GROUP: 95 children

I. *OBJECTIVES*

1. To help the child

    understand the people of Mexico.
    learn to appreciate the people of Mexico.
    learn how he can help the people of Mexico.
    compare the life of Mexico with that of the United States.
    learn to live with a culture different from his own.
    learn how Mexico helps the United States.
    learn how our government is different from that of Mexico.

II. *SUGGESTED ACTIVITIES FOR LARGE GROUPS (MOTIVATION)*

1. Film, filmstrips, slides
2. Transparencies
3. Maps and globes of Mexico
4. Resource persons
5. Pictures (Mexico)

6. Objects from Mexico
7. Mexican music
8. Mexican dances
9. Mexican food
10. Demonstrations (dances, role playing, folk songs)

III. *OUTLINE OF CONTENT*–(Usually presented in small groups or by individuals)

1. Location of Mexico
2. People (history)
3. Climate and seasons
4. Government (How it differs from that of the United States)
5. Industries (Kinds and possible expansions)
6. Natural resources (Water, soil, animals, plants, forest)
7. Recreation as compared to that in the United States
8. The Arts (Music, painting, crafts)
9. Education (Types of schools)
10. Geography (The land, rivers, lakes, mountains, etc.)
11. Money and banking in Mexico
12. Clothing, food, shelter
13. Language spoken
14. Religions and churches
15. Transportation (Land, air, water)
16. Communication

IV. *RESOURCES*–(MEDIA For Large and Small Groups)

1. Printed Material:

    Textbooks–on different levels (Readers, Histories, Geographies)
    Trade books–on different levels (Mexico)
    Magazines (Mexican, Holiday)
    Newspapers (New York Times, Mexican Newspapers)
    Charts, graphs, etc.
    Reference books (Mexican history)

2. Audio–Visual:

    Films on Mexico
    Filmstrips on Mexican Art
    Slides
    Transparencies–Maps of Mexico
    Maps and globes of Mexico

Resource persons
Music Instruments
Art Media
Recordings (Mexican Music—Hat Dance, etc.)

V. *CULMINATING ACTIVITIES* (For Large Groups or Small Groups)

1. Dramatics—Play developed by the group
2. Panel—News panel
3. Exhibit of the work completed
4. Skit illustrating a phase of the unit
5. Discussion groups
6. Written summary of the work
7. Creative writing and poetry concerning the unit
8. Seminar, debates, etc.
9. Mexican party and invite others

VI. *EVALUATION*

1. Teacher's observation of the work
2. Teacher's test for evaluating progress
3. Pupil evaluation of independent study
4. Checksheets of map skills, concepts learned, etc.
5. Standard tests

MODEL SCHEDULES FOR TEAM TEACHING

We propose a variety of team models for scheduling; several different types of schedules are possible. As many combinations are possible as there are team teaching programs since all schools are different.

Even more elaborate combinations would occur when the factors of nongrading are introduced within the team teaching approach.

The following questions should be considered when developing schedules for team teaching:

1. What are the needs of children?

2. What are the special talents of teachers?

3. What space is adequate for large groups, small groups, and individual instruction?

4. How are the children to be taught?

5. Who is to teach whom, and what is to be taught?

6. Will the schedule help implement the stated objectives?

7. Are the materials adequate for desirable learning experiences within the flexible schedule?

The schedule Model I on page 95 depicts the team staff members, the number of students, the time alloted, content areas to be taught, and planning periods for the team. Almost all content areas are scheduled during the same period enabling teachers to team. There is also a planning period each day from 2:30 to 3:15 when at least six teachers can plan cooperatively

The unique features of the team teaching schedule from Fairview Elementary School, Winston Salem, North Carolina, Model II, are: (1) that all groups plan and evaluate their daily activities from 2:15 − 2:30 each day; (2) music and physical education are taught to each grade level in a large group situation giving the team another opportunity to plan; (3) the language arts approach involves: reading, listening, speaking, writing, and spelling scheduled in a large block of time, enabling the team to integrate the language arts content; and (4) the language arts in grades one through six is scheduled from 8:20 − 10:30 each day enabling grade-level teams to cross content lines for inter-age grouping.

The McNeil Learning Center in Bowling Green, Kentucky divides their children into two divisions: Plaza A, primary children, and Plaza B, intermediate children. The team of teachers for each content area plan individualized prescribed packets. Children progress from packet to packet in a nongraded team teaching situation. On page 98 is a diagram, Model III, of spaces where the centers are located for individualized scheduling.

The chart on page 99, Model IV, illustrates the team teaching nongraded schedule for sixty-five primary age children in a rural school at East Stone Gap Elementary School, in Big Stone Gap, Virginia. As depicted in the schedule two teachers, one student teacher and two aides provide sufficient staff members to group the children in small groups by achievement in the skills areas: language arts, and mathematics. The schedule also provides for special

MODEL I
NONGRADED – TEAM TEACHING SEHEDULE
INTERMEDIATE LEVEL

Teacher	8:35-9:25	9:25-10:15	10:30-11:20	11:20-12:10	1:00-1:50	1:50-2:30	2:30-3:15
A	Soc. St. 4th - 44	Soc. St. 5th 27	Soc. St. 6th 36	plan	Eng. 24	Sp. Break 24	Supv. Study
B	Science 4th 50	Science 5th 28	Science 6th 37	plan	Eng. 21	Sp. & Break 21	Supv. Study
C	Reading 28	Reading 14	Math 17	Math 20	Eng. 28	Sp. & Break 21	plan
D	Reading 19	Reading 11	Math 16	Math 13	Eng. 28	Sp. & Break 28	plan
E	Reading 24	Reading 14	Math 16	Math 18	Eng. 28	Sp. & Break 27	plan
F	Reading 24	Reading 22	Math 20	Math 25	Eng. 34	Sp. & Break 34	plan
G	Reading 21	Reading 22	Math 15	Math 12	Eng. 31	Sp. & Break 31	plan
H	Reading 12	Reading 10	Math 10	Math 15	Eng. 29	Sp. & Break 29	plan
I				Math 25			
J				4th Library 47			4th Library 47
K		6th P.E. 73	5th P.E. 55	4th P.E. 47			4th P.E. 47
L							Music
M		P.E.	P.E.	Library			Library

224 Students   8 Teachers   1 Principal   1 P.E. Teacher
                  1 Librarian   2 Aides   1 Music Teacher

activities where the children can be regrouped again for individual help. In music, art, and physical education, the children are taught in both small class groups, and in large group situations, enabling the team to plan.

In this team teaching plan, the content subjects are scheduled so that children are grouped heterogeneously by age; they are regrouped in small groups and individually within this structure when the need arises.

The flexibility of this schedule provides for a large-block time schedule for skill development, enabling the utilization of a team of two teachers, a student teacher and aides for the grouping and regrouping of children; the principal and specialists also cooperate with this team and are a vital part of the total second year class team.

This school is an old building remodeled for team teaching; some of the walls have been removed and dividers provide for small group work.

The schedule on page 101, Model V, explains the special education schedule of Bob Byrd's special education class in Kingsport City Schools, Kingsport, Tennessee. This schedule illustrates modules of time for large groups, small groups, and individual instruction. It also depicts the use of specialists in the schedule; e.g.; art, music, and physical education, permitting the children from the special education class to be with other children of various backgrounds during part of the day.

The intermediate division of the Tusculum Elementary School is also a large area built for team teaching. This large space has movable furniture and mobile learning units; the floor area is also carpeted and the area joins the material center.

Since most of the child's work in this division is individualized, the team of intermediate teachers plan the prescribed program for each child.

On page 102 is a typical individualized schedule, Model VI. This schedule depicts the time blocks, the teacher in charge, and the content area where the child will work independently. In this situation, the teacher is more of a resource person. There are times when children meet in large and small group situations.

The schedule on page 103, Model VII, for the primary team teaching nongraded program at Tusculum Elementary School, Greenville, Tennessee, shows how content areas can be scheduled where large groups, small groups, and individuals can work together.

TEAM TEACHING

TEAM TEACHING MODEL II
FAIRVIEW ELEMENTARY SCHOOL, WINSTON SALEM, NORTH CAROLINA
MASTER SCHEDULE

	8:20	8:30	10:30	11:00	11:00 11:45	11:45 12:30	12:30	1:15	1:15	2:15	2:15	2:30
Gr. 1	O P E N	Language Arts Dev. Rdg. Spelling, Language, Writing, Speaking, Listening	10:30 11:00 Physical Education	Mathematics	Social Studies Current Events Social Living Science		Lunch	Music, Art, Story Hour, Sharing Films Creative Activity			E V A L	D I S
Gr. 2	I N G	Language Arts Dev. Rdg. Spelling Language, Writing Speaking, Listening	10:25 11:00 Mathematics		11:00 11:35 Lunch	11:35 12:30 Social Studies Current Events Social Living	12:30 1:00 Physical Education Large Group		1:00 - 1:30 Science Health Safety	1:30 - 2:15 Music Art, Films Story Hour Sharing	M A T I	M I S
Gr. 3	and	8:30 10:25 Language Arts Dev. Rdg. Spelling Language, Writing Speaking, Listening	10:25 11:15 Mathematics		11:15 11:50 Lunch	11:50 12:15 Science and Health	12:15 1:15 Social Studies Current Events Social Living		1:15 - 1:45 Physical Education Large Group	1:45 - 2:15 Music, Art Creative Activities	O N and	S A L
Gr. 4	R E	8:30 10:15 Language Arts Dev. Rdg. Spelling Language, Writing Speaking, Listening	10:15 10:45 Physical Education		10:45 11:40 Science and Health	11:40 12:15 Lunch	12:15 1:00 Mathematics		1:00 Social Studies World News, Art History, Geography Social Living, Music	2:15	P L A N	
Gr. 5	P R T S	8:30 10:30 Language Arts Dev. Rdg. Spelling Language, Writing Speaking, Listening	10:30 11:00 Physical Education		11:00 11:55 Mathematics	11:55 12:30 Lunch	12:30 1:15 Science and Health		1:15 Social Studies, Current Events, Art, Music, History, Geo. Social Living	2:15	N I	
Gr. 6	S	8:30 10:15 Language Arts Dev. Rdg. Spelling Language, Writing Speaking, Listening	10:15 10:45 Physical Education		10:45 11:35 Mathematics	11:35 12:15 Science and Health	12:15 12:50 Lunch		12:50 Social Studies World News, Art, Music History, Geography Social Living	2:15	N	
		Language Arts Dev. Rdg. Spelling Language, Writing Speaking			Mathematics	Science and Health	Lunch		Social Studies, World News Art, Music, History, Geo., Social Living		G	

Library—Grades 1, 2, 3, each meet once per week; grades 4, 5, 6, meet twice per week. ----- Music—String students from grades 5 and 6 meet once per week.
Music—All grades meet once per week. ----- Music Instrumental students from grades 5 and 6 meet once per week.
Remedial Reading and Speech students meet according to individual schedules.
Supervised Lunch is scheduled as a continuing lunch on separate schedule.

MODEL III
McNEIL INDIVIDUALIZED LEARNING CENTER
Bowling Green, Kentucky

Language Arts Learning Center		Resource-e-teria I	Observation	Reading and Science	Science Learning Center	Mathematics L.C.
Beginners	i/t/a	Observation	Reading Enrichment	Beginners	Plaza A	Mathematics L.C.
Mathematics Learning Center		Observation	Observation	Music		Social Studies
Science Learning Center		Observation	Observation	Language Arts	Plaza B	Social Studies
Living Science Laboratory						Plaza A
Curateria		Language Arts Learning Center	Resource-e-teria	Faculty Lounge	Entrance	Art / P.E. Multi-purpose
Title III Office	Learning Program Directors	Learning Center Coordinator	Reading Enrichment			Kitchen

TEAM TEACHING

MODEL IV
TEAM TEACHING - NONGRADED APPROACH
EAST STONE GAP ELEMENTARY SCHOOL, BIG STONE GAP, VIRGINIA
PRIMARY CHILDREN

	8:45-10:15	10:30-11:30	11:30-12:00	12:00-1:15	1:15-2:00	2:00-2:40	2:40-3:20
	Language Art	Math	Lunch	Special Activities	Soc. Studies Health & Science	P.E. & Music	Special Act. SRA, Films, filmstrips Skill development
2nd Aide				33 T & F (R) 32 M & TH (D)		T & F (R) M & TH (D)	Films, Filmstrips, Skills
Duff				32 T, W, F	32	32 T & F	32
Robinette	Student G	S. Teacher		33 M, W, TH S. Teacher	33	33 M & TH	33
Carter 1st Aide					W(gym) M,T, TH,F Duff 2nd	M, TH 1st-Reach	M, TH Duff
McCoy 2nd Aide					M,T, TH, F Robinette	M, TH, 1st. Stallard (gym) W	M, TH Robinette
Carter 1st Aide							
Cornett & Bailey						65	
Bailey						T & F (D) M, TH (R)	

| 2 Teachers | 2 Aides | 1 Art | 65 Children |
| 1 Student Teacher | 1 P. E. Teacher | 1 Music | |

To Be Served in the Rooms

These primary children are grouped in one large area in a modern, flexible building designed for team teaching. The area is carpeted and open, therefore, the children can move freely from area to area within the large primary division. Here the children work at their own rate in a nongraded program. The children are grouped and regrouped within the large area for various reasons. The teachers work cooperatively as a team to plan, implement, and evaluate the program.

Since the children move from area to area within the large group situation in the primary division, it is essential that each child has his own individualized schedule. The schedule on page 104, Model VIII, is a typical one for a primary child in the Tusculum View Elementary School.

Model IX is an individual schedule divided into twenty-minute modules. With the help of his teacher, the counselor, or a trained aide, the child schedules his work at the beginning of each week. He will spend as many modules as needed in each content area. Music, art, and physical education are a part of the total school schedule. This schedule is shown on page 105.

SUMMARY

In summary, team teaching is utilized to share the talents of teachers with a group of children for improved instruction. Nevertheless, each of them should bear special responsibilities for the welfare of one portion of the group, that is for a complete "class."

The team works together to develop plans for instruction, and then determines together the best way in which each teacher's talents can be used in the realization of their plans. Finally, they evaluate together the progress made by the pupils.

MODEL V
SPECIAL EDUCATION

TEACHER OR SUBJECT: *Special Education - Explanation of schedule:*
Special Education Teacher
Physical Education

TEAM, NUMBER TWO: *Music*
Art

LG. Large Group
1st Digit - Group
2nd Digit - Group

Module	1	2	3	4	5	6	7	8	9	10	11	12	13	14
Starting Time	8:30	9:00	9:30	10:00	10:30	11:00	11:30	12:00	12:30	1:00	1:30	2:00	2:30	3:00
Monday	SHOP			READING			Lunch	HEALTH		PHYSICAL EDC.				
Tuesday	SHOP	Large Group Arts			AND		Lunch		AND	VOCATIONAL				
Wednesday	SHOP			LANGUAGE	ARTS		Lunch	PERSONAL HABITS		MATHEMATICS		AND		
Thursday	SHOP	Large Group Music					Lunch					NUMBER		
Friday	SHOP						Lunch			PHYSICAL EDC.		CONCEPTS		

101

MODEL VI
INDIVIDUAL STUDENT SCHEDULE
TUSCULUM VIEW SCHOOL
GREENVILLE, TENNESSEE

Name _____

	Thompson	Frady	Gout	Casteel	Cate	Johnson
8:00-8:55	Language Arts					
8:55-9:40				Math		
9:40-10:30						Science
10:30-11:15			Physical Education			
11:15-12:00	Lunch		Lunch		Lunch	
12:00-12:55			Social Studies			
12:55-1:50	Exploratory Period in any area of individual interest or time may be spent in giving individual assistance to younger children.					
1:50-2:45		Language Arts				

TEAM TEACHING

MODEL VII
TUSCULUM VIEW SCHOOL
PRIMARY SCHEDULE

*SPECIAL EDUCATION

TIME	TEACHER A	TEACHER B	TEACHER C	TEACHER D	TEACHER E	TEACHER F	TEACHER G
8:00 8:45	Language Arts	Language Arts	Language Arts	Language Arts	Break	Science Health	Language* Arts
8:45 9:30	Language Arts	Language Arts	Language Arts	Language Arts	Math	Break	Language Arts
9:30 10:15	Language Arts	Language Arts	Break	Language Arts	Math	Science Health	Language Arts
10:15 11:00	Language Arts	Language Arts	Language Arts	Break	Math	Science Health	Language Arts
11:00 11:45	Lunch	Lunch	Lunch	Lunch	Lunch	Lunch	Lunch
11:45 12:30	Language Arts	Language Arts	Language Arts	Language Arts	Math	Science Health	Science Health
12:30 1:15	Physical Education	Physical Eductaion	Physical Education	Physical Education	Physical Education	Physical Education	Break
1:15 2:00	Social Studies	Break	Social Studies	Language Arts	Math	Science Health	Math
2:00 2:45	Break	Social Studies	Social Studies	Social Studies	Math	Science Studies	Social Studies

MODEL VIII
INDIVIDUAL SCHEDULE FOR CHILD
TUSCULUM VIEW ELEMENTARY PRIMARY DIVISION

Time	Chamberlain	Hunter	Bradley	Griffin	Hashe	Johnson	Springfield	Library
8:00-8:45	Reading Penmanship							
8:45-9:30	Reading							
9:30-10:15				English				
10:15-11:00			Spelling					
11:00-11:45	Lunch	Lunch	Lunch	Lunch	Lunch	Lunch	Lunch	Lunch
11:45-12:30					Math			
12:30-1:15	P.E.	P.E.	P.E.	P.E.	P.E.	P.E.	P.E.	P.E.
1:15-2:00						Science Health		
2:00-2:45		Social Studies						

MODEL IX TYPICAL INDIVIDUAL SCHEDULE

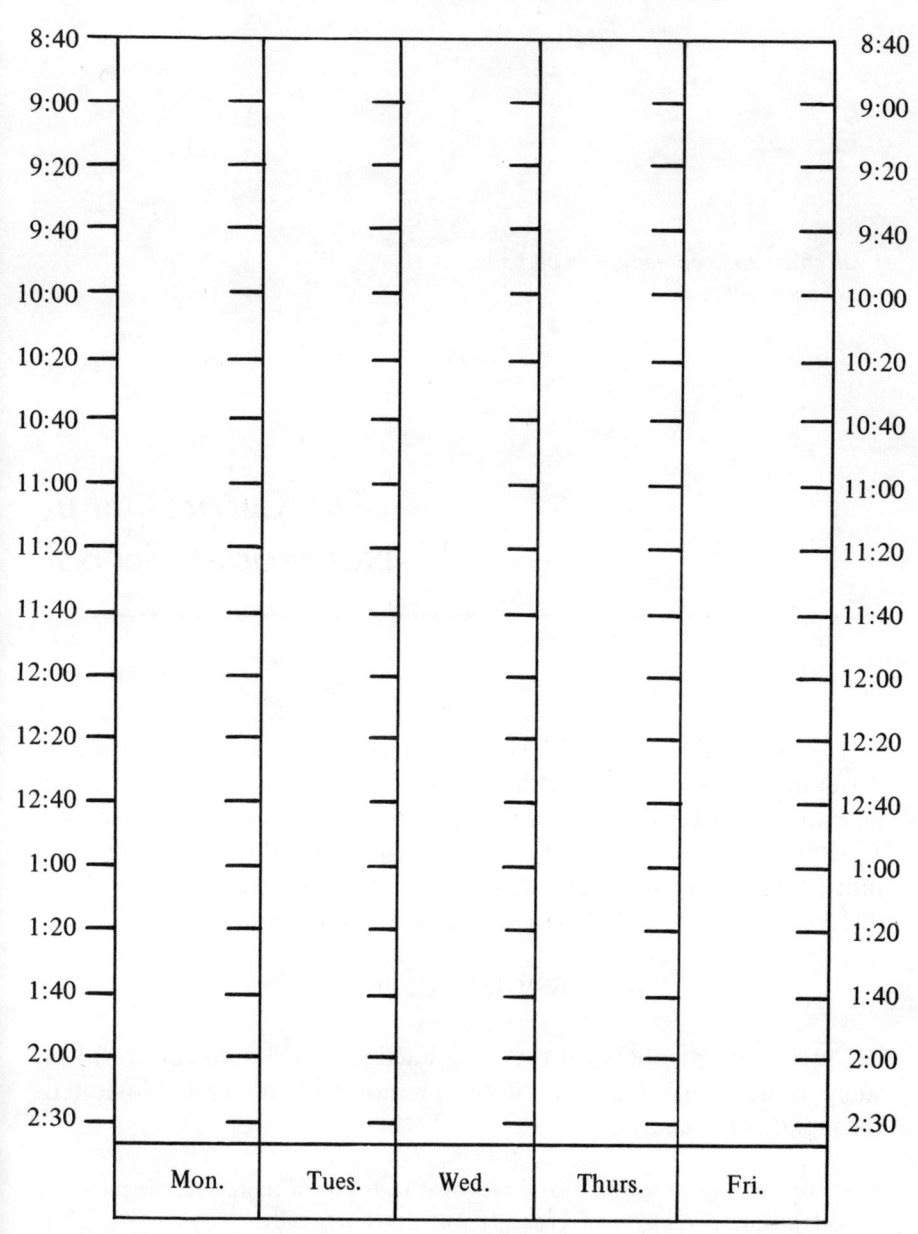

	Mon.	Tues.	Wed.	Thurs.	Fri.
8:40					
9:00					
9:20					
9:40					
10:00					
10:20					
10:40					
11:00					
11:20					
11:40					
12:00					
12:20					
12:40					
1:00					
1:20					
1:40					
2:00					
2:30					

Name: _____
Total Time Spent In the Following Content Areas:
Social Studies _____ Science _____ Language Arts _____ Math _____

I will study and get ready, and perhaps my chance will come.

               Lincoln

5

The Curriculum in the Nongraded School

The nongraded school is purposely designed to care for individual differences. As an administrative means for organizing learners and learning opportunities, the nongraded school is characterized by its flexibility. Thus, flexibility is derived from the recognition of individual differences significant to the learning process. Such differences mandate differences in educational practices.

PROFESSIONAL OBJECTIVES

Curriculum planners for the nongraded school should aim to fulfill such basic objectives as those presented here and illustrated throughout the chapter.

1. To develop programs that have great concern for individual progress: academically, physically, socially, and psychologically.

2. To provide opportunities for children to learn and make progress according to their own ability.

3. To organize learning experiences which provide opportunities for children to learn through self-discovery and individual exploration.

4. To develop units in behavioral sciences giving children increased opportunity to learn about themselves as human beings.

5. To consider experiences for children which will enhance the self-concept of each child; experience and conditions which most likely foster behavioral freedom where knowledge of self and environment are recognized as co-extensive.

6. To eliminate promotion barriers in attempting to remove some of the psychological stresses.

7. To provide report forms which attempt to evaluate individual personal growth and progress in the academic areas based on an estimate of the child's ability rather than a standard norm.

8. To provide broader understanding of the staff toward the learning process, and how it prevails all learning and living experiences in school-program content, child-adult relations, and methods of guiding and measuring achievement.

9. To provide curriculum experiences geared toward understanding of concepts, processes and meanings in contrast to rote memorization of facts and principles.

It cannot be overstated that these objectives along with others become prime considerations for curriculum planners organizing nongraded schools. It is not the grouping that makes the difference, it is what happens to the child while being grouped and regrouped in the flexible school.

Goodlad analyzed classes at different grade levels and reached several important generalizations about the pupil realities or developmental processes with which teachers must deal when planning learning experiences for children:

1. Children enter the first grade with a range of from three to four years in their readiness to profit from a "graded minimum essentials" concept of schooling.

2. This initial spread in abilities increases over the years so that it is approximately double this amount by the time children approach the end of elementary school.

3. The achievement range among pupils begins to approximate the range in intellectual readiness to learn soon after first-grade children are exposed to reasonably normal school instruction.

4. Differing abilities, interests, and opportunities among children cause the range in certain specific attainments to surpass the range in general achievement.

5. Individual children's achievement patterns differ markedly from learning area to learning area.

6. By the time children reach the intermediate elementary grades, the range in intellectual readiness to learn and in most areas of achievement is as great as or greater than the number designating the grade level.[1]

CONSIDERATIONS OF WHAT TO TEACH

The modern curriculum which is characterized in the nongraded school is marked by updating the content, some new approaches to methodology, and a reorganization of subject matter.

Curriculum planners in the nongraded program organize their learning experiences around structural elements of the discipline e.g., key ideas, principles and concepts. To understand these elements, it gives the students intellectual power to attack unfamiliar problems as well as understand phenomena already experienced.

What is new in the curriculum with considerations of what to teach follow:

Language Arts

There is more concern for oral language activities which enable children to talk and discuss rather than recite.

The children are involved in listening and speaking to one another in natural settings and on issues which concern them. Many of these

---

[1] John I. Goodlad and Robert H. Anderson, *The Nongraded Elementary School*. (New York: Harcourt, Brace and Company, 1959), pp. 27-28.

settings should bring children together from various backgrounds for study and discussion.

The structure of language is being stressed, involving a study of linguistics.

There is interest in expanding the language arts into the humanities, combining music, art, and literature, helping to insure relationships already present among these areas.

As with all new content, mass media has found its place in the language arts program through the use of tapes for listening; films, and filmstrips for reading and viewing; programmed materials, teaching machines, and computers for developing phonetic skills, word recognition, comprehension, and listening skills.

Paperback books, tradebooks, and reference materials of various types appropriate for different levels of the child's development have also flooded the schools for individualizing the total language arts program—listening, speaking, reading, and writing.

Mathematics

Skills in mathematics should be taught in a variety of ways thus giving each child an opportunity to master them according to his own learning style. As the skills are mastered, spiral development of the curriculum becomes a reality.

The following are some important considerations in planning a mathematics program for the nongraded school:

1. The numeric theme is to develop the structure of the number system beginning with counting numbers in the kindergarten.

2. Stress should be placed on the functional concepts as a means of unifying mathematical ideas which are central to many areas of mathematics.

3. Algebra and geometry should be moved closer together and begin with a readiness in the early years of a child's schooling.

4. Logical reasons as well as deductive methods are emphasized throughout the program.

5. Computer-oriented concepts are utilized.

6. Probability and statistics should be taught throughout the upper levels.

7. There should be stress on the structure of mathematics, unifying ideas, (sets), variables, functions, and relations.

Science

Science for the children in the modern nongraded school stresses children's activities. These learning experiences attempt to communicate the nature of science as inquiry.

The science experiences are organized to create interest and develop concepts achieved beyond those taught by the use of traditional textbook teaching.

The new science programs being developed stress those overlapping the mathematic program, combining physical and life science, and stress the process approach—reading, observing, classifying, experimenting, and recording data.

Science content which is more adaptable in individual differences is more appropriate for the nongraded school. It should enhance the inquiry approach since the inquiry thread runs through all areas of the nongraded curriculum.

Science offers excellent opportunities for children to work in broad units of study built around major content areas. During these experiences scientific methods and attitudes should be examined. Basic scientific concepts should include (1) man's concept of truth changes as he changes and his environment changes; (2) there are interrelated causes for every natural event; and (3) man uses scientific discoveries to improve his daily living.

The following science units are appropriate for a group of children during their fourth year of school:

1. How plants grow; how we depend upon them

2. Learning more about the earth

3. Learning to know more about the air around us

4. Understanding the space age

5. Knowing about matter and energy

6. Animals and their role in nature

7. Safety in our community and nation

THE CURRICULUM

8. How to keep our bodies strong and healthy

9. Machines that work for us

For the benefit of those children who will need more time to achieve the goals of the elementary science program, units may be added to reinforce the understandings of previous units. The children who are able to move ahead will find the units of the next year or phase challenging.

Other schools are individualizing their science programs through programmed material, science kits, and/or packets. The McNeil Learning Center, Bowling Green, Kentucky individualized their science program through learning packets, using a laboratory for experimenting and research work. Children progress from phase to phase in science through this nongraded approach.

The following illustrates a packet used in science in the Primary Division of the Modern Elementary School, Norton, Virginia.

SILENCE AND SOUND

Hi Boys and Girls,

We are going to have new experiences with silence and sound. We hope that you will become aware of different sounds around you and discover how they are produced.

Science Staff
Norton City School

We cannot ⊙ ⊙ sound.
We cannot touch sound.
We can only ⓠ sound.
We need sound.

HOW

?

Norton City School   Grade 2

SILENCE AND SOUND

How Sounds Are Made
Objective 1. Sound is a result of something moving. This is called vibration.

1. Plane — Underline the sound made by a moving plane.
   (roar, blow, road)

2. Car — Underline the sound made by a moving car.
   (ring, rumble, trick)

3. dog — Underline the sound made by a dog.
   (lark, mark, bark)

4. Look at page 40 in *Concepts in Science*.
   Can sounds be made by plucking, blowing and rubbing: Yes or No

STOP Ask your coordinator to check your work.

Objective 2. That moving things make different sounds.

1. bell — What must be done to get sound from a bell?
   (show, shake, shade)

THE CURRICULUM

2.  What must be done to get a sound from a drum?
(meat, beat, seat)

3.  What must be done to get sound from a ball?
(bounce, shout, float)

Look on page 41 in *Concepts in Science*.
1. What makes a ringing sound?
2. What makes a booming sound?
3. What makes a shrill sound?

STOP Ask your coordinator to check your work.

Objective 3. Sound from string instruments is produced by moving strings.

1.  We make sound from a guitar by (picking, rubbing, hitting) the strings.

2.  We make sounds from a violin by (picking, rubbing, hitting) the bow over the strings.

3.  We make sound from a piano by (picking, rubbing, hitting) the keys.

1. Read page 42 in *Concepts in Science.* Answer the two questions.
2. What do you hear when strings of musical instruments do not vibrate?
3. Do all musical instruments have strings?

STOP Ask your coordinator to check your work.

Objective 4. Sound can be made from instruments that do not have strings.

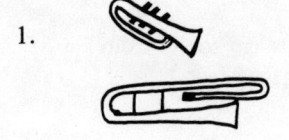

1. Turn to page 130 in *Childcraft,* Vol. 8. These are wind instruments. How do they make sound?

2. Turn to page 43 in *Concepts in Science.* Read.

1. We get sounds from horns by _____ into the horn.
2. The moving air vibrates and makes _____ .
3. We can hit the drum to make _____ .
4. Hitting makes the drum vibrate and then we have _____ .
5. How is sound made from horns and drums? _____ and _____ .

STOP Ask your coordinator to check your work.

Objective 5. Sounds vary in pitch; they may be high or low.

Cricket   Frog   Turn to page 20 in *Sound* by Russell. Read page 20. Then answer questions.

1. How are high sounds made?
2. How are low sounds made?
3. How does a cricket make a high sound?
4. How does a bullfrog make a deep sound?
5. Are all sounds alike?

THE CURRICULUM

6. Why do small things make high sounds?
7. Why do large things make low sounds?

STOP Ask your coordinator to check your work.
Do investigate on page 46 in *Concepts in Science* with teacher or aide.
STOP

Objective 6. Sound travels through solids, liquids, or gases.

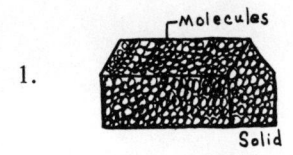

1. In wood, molecules are close together.
    Read pages 10-12 in *Sound* by Neal.

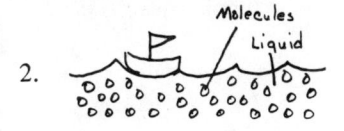

2. In liquids molecules are far apart.

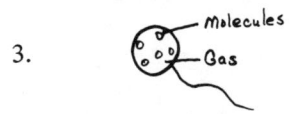

3. In air molecules are very very far apart.

1. Sound travels fastest in solids, such as _____ and _____ .
2. The molecules are very close together in _____ .
3. Sound travels the slowest in water or air.
4. What carries the vibrations in sound?

STOP Ask your coordinator to check your work.

Objective 7. Extending concept through investigation.

Read pages 140-144 in *In Your Neighborhood.*
Now do the experiments on pages 143 and 144.

116   THE CURRICULUM

STOP Have experiments checked by teacher's aide.

Objective 8. What did I remember about sound?

Answer four questions on page 146 in *In Your Neighborhood.*
Also go over things to remember on page 146.

STOP Ask your coordinator to check your work.

Objective 9. Discover how sound travels.

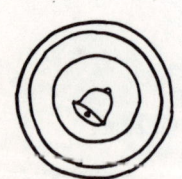

Read pages 10-12.
Sound waves ∿∿ in book called *Sound* by Russell.
How does sound go from the bell to your ear?

1. Did you find out that sound travels in wave patterns?
2. Sound can travel through solids (wood), liquids (water), or gases (air).
3. How are sounds made?
4. How does sound travel?
5. Can you see sound?

STOP Ask your coordinator to check your work.

Objective 10. Discover how sound travels.

Read pages 18-20, in *Sound* by Miller.

Does sound come through closed doors and windows?

THE CURRICULUM   117

Read pages 21 and 22 in *Sound* by Miller.
Can sound be made under the water?

Read pages 22-24.
Does sound travel the fastest in gases? Why or why not?

1. Write down sounds you hear now.

STOP Ask your coordinator to check your work.

Objective 11. Sound travels in wave patterns through molecules of solids, liquids, or gases.

Read page 48 in *Concepts in Science.*
How do we hear?

Read page 49 in *Concepts in Science.*
What happens if sound waves do not reach the ear?

Objective 12. Speech is a sound pattern

Read page 50 in *Concepts in Science.*
What happens when Bob spoke?
When does Tom hear?

THE CURRICULUM

Read pages 14 and 15 in *Sound* by Miller.
Describe sound waves.

Objective 13. Reflection of sound waves.

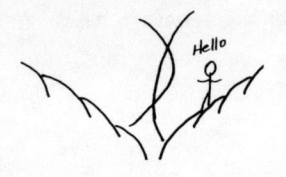

Read page 51 in *Concepts in Science*.
What kind of things can reflect sound?
What makes an echo?

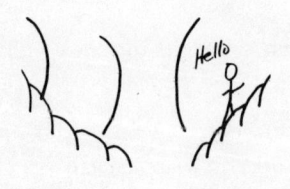

What happens when a sound is reflected?
Does the sound wave make a two-way trip?

Read page 26 in *Sounds*.
Why did the sound wave come back?

1. How do sound waves travel. Hit a hard smooth surface and bounce back, what do you hear?

STOP Ask your coordinator to check your paper.

Objective 14. Hearing Sounds

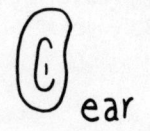

Read page 52 in *Concepts in Science*.
What collects sound?

THE CURRICULUM 119

How does sound get to the eardrum?
What makes the eardrum vibrate? See page 52.

Look at diagram page 52

Find the parts of the ear.
What is at the inside end of the canal? See page 52.

1. What does the eardrum do?
2. What do the tiny bones do?
3. What do we call the part of the ear that collects sound?

STOP Have your paper checked.

Do investigation on pages 53 and 54 in *Concepts in Science.*

Check your findings with the teacher or aide.

Objective 15. Sound does not travel through a vacuum.

Read in Concepts in Science See Page 55

Here we are on the moon.
Do we have air?

Read
Page 55

How do the men breathe?
What are they carrying?
What is in the tanks that they are carrying?

Would you hear a plane or car on the moon?
Why or why not?

THE END

Check your paper.

Silence and sound have been fun.

VOCABULARY

vibrate	echo
strings	reflect
sound waves	bounce
molecules	diagram
solids	outer ear
liquids	canal
gases	bones
silence	eardrum

SILENCE AND SOUND

Bibliography

Baker, Maddux, Warrin, *In Your Neighborhood*
Brandwein, Cooper, Blackwood, Hone, *Concepts in Science,* Harcourt Brace and World, Inc. 1966, pp. 40-56
Childcraft, *How Things Are Made,* Vol. 8, pages 106-146.
Kohn, Bernice, *Echoes,* Coward-McCann, Inc. 1965.
Miller, Lisa, *Sound,* Coward-McCann, Inc. 1965.
Neal, Charles, *Sound,* Follett Publishing Co.
Russell, B. J., *Sound,* Bobbs-Merrill

THE CURRICULUM

Social Studies

Some nongraded schools have developed comprehensive K-12 social studies programs with an interdisciplinary or multidisciplinary base. Others are concerned with specific units which draw upon multiple disciplines. Others work with a multidisciplinary base to deal with broad themes or problem areas, such as intergroup relations.

The following factors are considered important in deciding what to teach in the social studies program:

1. Many experimental social studies programs introduce geographic concepts in the elementary grades, the new stress being placed on man and his environment; place geography is not being stressed.

2. The place of history declines since the emphasis is placed on social skills and social reality; humanization is the keynote.

3. Economic concepts are stressed at an earlier age.

4. Political science content has been expanded and revamped in the modern curriculum and stresses such concepts as conflict, authority, justice and law, civil rights, the behavior of different countries, and political processes.

5. A world view approach in history is presented in the modern curriculum.

6. The use of multi-media is essential, recognizing that no social studies textbook is adequate.
    Content in social studies becomes a vehicle for developing process goals, such as the learner's ability to engage in planning, organizing, and making decisions. This suggests that it makes no difference what topics, areas of study, or themes are choosen for study in the nongraded school. The emphasis on process and concepts may be the most significant aspect of the search for relevancy in developing content for the nongraded social studies program.

The following content in social studies may provide a guide for problem areas of study for a child during his third year in school.

1. Learning to know our community
   a. History
   b. Location
   c. Climate
   d. People
   e. Work
   f. Recreation
   g. Products

2. Where We Get Our Food, Shelter and Clothing
   a. Kinds of foods
   b. Kinds of homes
   c. Kinds of clothing

3. Protecting the Natural Resources in Our Community and State
   a. Animals
   b. Plants
   c. Water
   d. Minerals
   e. Human Resources

4. Communication and Transportation to and from Our City
   a. Telephone
   b. Radio
   c. Television
   d. Mail
   e. Telegraph
   f. Trains and Rail Routes
   g. Buses and bus routes
   h. Airplanes and air routes
   i. Automobiles and road routes

5. Great American Heroes in
   a. Literature
   b. History
   c. Nature
   d. Inventions
   e. Social Services
   f. Government
   g. Poetry

6. Utilities and Services
   a. Electricity for Power and Light
   b. Water for Use

THE CURRICULUM

    c. Gasoline for Power
    d. Gas for Fuel
    e. Health and Sanitation
    f. Safety Protection

7. A Big City—New York
    a. Kinds of people
    b. Population
    c. Location
    d. Climate
    e. Industries
    f. Scenic Places
    g. Historical Places

8. London—Another Great Metropolitan Area Overseas
    a. Kinds of people
    b. Population
    c. Location
    d. Climate
    e. Industries
    f. Scenic Places
    g. Historical Places

9. Parks and Recreation
    a. Types of Activities
    b. Location
    c. Importance of Play and Rest

10. A Rural Town
    a. Kinds of People
    b. Location
    c. Scenic Places
    d. Kind of Stores
    e. Recreation

For the benefit of those children who will need more time to achieve the goals of the elementary social studies program, units may be added to reinforce the understandings of the previous units.

Some schools use independent study as a means of progressing through the nongraded school.

Health and Physical Education

Not many teachers will be called upon to teach physical

education. It will be taught by teachers who have had specialized training for teaching the subject.

There are really three different purposes in teaching physical education. One is to make participants of pupils, to build strong bodies and good health habits, and to make better consumers of the products—such as, the balls, the field, the clothing. If we want children to accomplish the above objectives in physical education, they must have many opportunities to create their own participation, and to enjoy their products in their own unique way.

The health program has as its ultimate goal the development of the social, emotional, and physical needs of the child. The listed instructional areas following strive to develop a well-planned and directed instructional health and safety program which will provide satisfying and enriching experiences for the elementary school child.

Any good health and physical education program for the elementary school will include large group, small group, and individual experiences in the following areas:

1. *Body dynamics.* Activities that emphasize vigorous use of large muscle groups.

2. *Story plays.* Activities in story form that emphasize the imitative actions, natural and spontaneous, that are related to child growth and development.

3. *Rhythms.* Activities of creative and interpretive type to develop a balanced, well-coordinated body.

4. *Singing games.* Games involving singing and pantomime through which mastery of certain skills, poise, and enjoyment are achieved.

5. *Dances.* Dances which provide rich cultural, social, and recreational experiences.

6. *Stunts.* Activities of self-testing, that involve body exercise and control, that develop strength, flexibility and coordination.

7. *Games.* Activities which involve running, skipping, chasing, hopping, jumping and standing.

8. *Relays.* These involve races and team play.

THE CURRICULUM 125

9. *Sex Education.* Information what will enable the child to understand himself.

10. *Food, Clothing, Shelter.* Activities enabling the child to live a healthy and safe life.

11. *Study of Medicine and Diseases.* Information concerning the prevention, cause, and cure of diseases.

12. *Safety.* Activities that teach safety in the home, school, community, and world.

It must be kept in mind while providing experiences in health and safety that the ultimate goal is the development of the whole child. All activities should strive to develop a well-planned and directed instructional program of health and safety which will provide satisfying and enriching experiences for the child.

Grouping children for health and safety experiences must take into consideration the realization of individual differences in the social, emotional, and physical development of each child. Activities and experiences must help to develop self-expression, encourage the child to participate in groups, and build healthy bodies of each individual. This calls for grouping and regrouping of children to meet their basic needs.

The Arts

The program for creative arts will encourage the creative self-realization of children. The arts have a high potential for integrating meanings which emerge from social experiences. For this reason, the arts are readily coordinated with social studies and language arts, deepening and intensifying the knowledge and sensitivity gained about people and their modes of living and ways of thinking.

The teachers motivate, guide, encourage, appreciate, and support the children toward creative self-realization.

The teachers with the help of specialists cooperate to encourage and support the creative arts which will encounter the whole continuum from repetitive to creative experiences in the arts.

Art and music are intimately associated with the child's personality. The nongraded program provides a setting for integrating the overlapping stages of pupil maturity.

Learning experiences in art for a child in the primary school might include the following:

1. Individual painting and group mural projects with crayon, tempera, and mixed media.

2. Using many kinds of paper cutting, teasing, combining and assembling.

3. Mosaics, applying the design principles learned in drawing and painting.

4. Modeling and building in clay.

5. Constructing with papier-mâché.

6. Wood and wire construction.

7. Using mixed media in cloth, beads, string, wood, wire, and foil.

8. Creative illustrations of stories, events, and ideas from their daily work.

9. Opportunities to engage in and experiment with creative movement.

Every attempt should be made to include all areas of experience in developing the pupil's musical background. Music activities for a child in the nongraded school should include the following experiences:

1. Listening experiences with emphasis on suitable pitch, tempo, rhythm, and tone.

2. Singing appropriate songs with emphasis on suitable pitch, tempo, rhythm, and tone.

3. Experimenting with simple rhythm and melody instruments.

4. Singing appropriate songs correlated with other aspects of the teaching program.

5. Emphasis on recognition and expression of fundamental rhythmic patterns.

6. Identification of music symbols and the rise and fall of melodic line.

7. Creative activities with songs, instruments, and movements.

THE CURRICULUM

HOW THE CONTENT SHOULD BE TAUGHT

In planning how the content should be taught in the nongraded school it will be important to diagnose the learning style of each child, and adapt the learning experience to his style. This adjustment has come closer to us as we have begun to analyze how children learn, especially those coming from different cultures as well as deprived environments. Planning instructional objectives around the learning pattern of the child has become the greatest challenge of the nongraded school. This planning makes different demands on the team teachers, aides, and specialists.

There will be a concern for writing behavioral objectives which are appropriate for each child; there will be a clearer diagnosis also of each child to see that he is accomplishing the prescribed objectives. The behavioral objectives presented here are examples of objectives you might use in a reading program.

_____ _____Given twenty unmatched pairs of rhyming words the child can correctly match thirteen of the pairs

_____When given orally by the teacher or on tape a list of fifteen words, one at a time, the child can supply a rhyming word for nine of the words

The child can orally give the teacher two words which begin with each of the following single initial consonants:

_____ b
_____ d
_____ f
_____ h
_____ j
_____ k
_____ l
_____ m
_____ n
_____ p
_____ q
_____ r
_____ s
_____ t
_____ v
_____ w

_____ x
_____ y
_____ z

_____ When given a list of twenty words containing initial blends the child can name the initial blends in fourteen of the words

When given a story to read the child correctly answers direct questions as to:

a. _____ when
b. _____ where
c. _____ what
d. _____ why
e. _____ who
f. _____ how
(seventy-five percent accuracy)

Curriculum planners for the nongraded school must be concerned with whether or not children can handle a concept-oriented and process-oriented curriculum. Will they continue to be interested, and will they be self-motivated?

Another challenge to curriculum planners as they decide how the content should be taught is how to adjust newer approaches in curriculum to the varied population. Adaption is more than a faster or slower pace through the same material, or variations of instructional materials, the utilization of staff, or the way children are grouped. It is knowing what to prescribe for a child considering his physical, emotional, intellectual, and social development.

There will be less rigid skill assignments as well as concept expectations from particular levels or groups of children. Decisions on skill development or allocations of content and material are made with attention to more factors than just the subject matter itself. While objectives are set down for the group there is usually an agreement among the team members and others which states that some children will not work up to the prescribed attainments for the group while others will progress much faster. Growth will continue and at each child's own rate of speed.

In the nongraded school it is necessary that instructional activity be provided to help children master the skills and competencies that they will need for entry into the occupational world. These experiences should be relevant to the occupational needs of a large majority of youth. These experiences may revolve around a cluster of concepts of vocational education providing a broad experience through the study of the world of work using multi-media, field trips, lectures, and group guidance as instructional aides.

INCLUDING SCOPE AND SEQUENCE IN THE CURRICULUM

When a whole staff, or any team of specialists selected from a staff, sets out to design and structure—then implement—its own nongraded program, it is necessary that the scope and sequence of what is *to be taught, to whom,* and *when,* be both considered and arranged for at each step and in terms of the total program. This requires that someone, usually the principal or an appropriate supervisor, act as a coordinator of the efforts of the various planning teams. The function of the coordinator, in this instance, being to see to it that several criteria of good program building are not violated in planning the necessary and desirable differentiation into the total program. A few criteria of this nature built into the nongraded school program follow:

1. When a skill is taught or learned at one level, is there sufficient opportunity to practice or reinforce it at a sufficient number of higher levels?

2. In vertical or sequential subject areas, does each level or unit really contain the essential background for mastering the next?

3. Where there is unit teaching, as in social studies, do the units planned cover the content planned for the child's total program?

4. How often do very similar units re-appear and why is it that way? Is it intentional for reinforcement and/or desirable enrichment or is it because teachers simply want to teach these units?

5. How is the effectiveness of the whole program to be determined? Are the measuring instruments, the reporting processes, and the bases of grading appropriate to the content and teaching methods used?

6. What provisions have been made for changing the program? That is, have the planners designed and written down the steps of the process for change?

7. Does the plan contain adequate provision for acquiring, using, and maintaining the equipment necessary to make it work?

These are the kinds of questions that need to be asked about the whole program and about each segment of it. Under the nongraded plan, the curriculum planning function, formerly carried out by the authorities who wrote and published the text books, falls directly into the hands of the school staff. In today's schools, you, the professionally certificated teachers, have had basic preparation for curriculum development. Planning improved local programs offers you an excellent opportunity to test your knowledge and ability. The vast amount of media published adds to this experience, also.

None of the previously mentioned ideas of this book are intended to suggest that the practically "guaranteed scope and sequence" planned into textbook courses is not still important. The shift, however, is that the determination of these things and the guarantee that respectability is maintained becomes a staff responsibility, under the coordination of a principal or an appropriate supervisor. This is why it becomes imperative that the whole faculty participate in the planning of the broad outlines of the whole program and that the details of operation be left to smaller teaching teams or teaching area specialists.

ELIMINATING ARTIFICIAL SUBJECT MATTER DIVISIONS

Standard subject matter divisions can be artificial if established merely for convenience. There is a need to integrate learning experiences through combining associated and interdependent content from all areas into broad learning units.

The teacher in the flexible elementary school should be able to combine knowledge from several sources which is essential in small group discussions, seminars, and team planning situations. For example, the language arts area should include reading, writing, listening, speaking, and spelling. The health, science, and safety areas should often be combined in order to make the concepts appear more meaningful. Generalizations in social studies should evolve from several disciplines, e.g., anthropology, history, geography, political science, economics, and civics. Arts and music should be integrated when possible to promote concept development. Mathematics should be based on meaningful theory and include functional experiences so that the child may explore, discover, and invent. Elementary

THE CURRICULUM

economics should be introduced in the first year of school, applying the mathematical and economical concepts in social experiences. Mathematics and science should also be correlated when possible.

Artificial subject matter lines can be eliminated especially when schedules are flexible, e.g., large blocks of time, modular scheduling, and seminars. It is imperative to use broad areas of study, cutting across content areas and grade lines since curriculum combinations are found to be applicable in the elementary nongraded team teaching school. The staff determines the educational goals, the content to be taught, who shall teach it, and where it shall be taught, therefore, it is imperative to integrate learning experiences.

ORGANIZING FOR INSTRUCTION

As stated in Chapter Two of this book, identifying children for instructional groups is essential. The staff must consider the data available for each child and with the help of the guidance counselor, school psychologist, team members, specialists, and curriculum director, plan an educational program which will insure progress for the child toward the proposed goals.

The total staff must cooperate in developing curricular material to be used in initiating the behavioral science sequence that are appropriate to the learning style of each child.

Children and parents should be consulted and made an integral part of the curriculum planning team, thus assuring their cooperation toward the proposed learning experiences.

Children will be placed in flexible instructional groups appropriate for their learning rate, interest, and talents. Teachers, specialists, and aides shall observe developmental patterns of behavior connected with the self-concept and self-agency factors. It is hoped that they will gain some insight in how to work with the individuals of different sex, intelligence, and socio-economic backgrounds.

When the curriculum is built around learning experiences, there is no necessary reason why each child should go through a sequence in isolation which will eliminate the opportunity for important social interaction. At any point in time, it is likely that within the nongraded school a group of students will be roughly at similar points in some of the same learning sequences. Therefore, they may be taught as a group.

At times children should be grouped together, especially in social studies, the arts, and in health and physical education. Here they can learn from each other, share experiences, plan together, and learn to appreciate the background of each member of the group.

Flexibility is the keynote when deciding to group children in the nongraded school; children will be grouped and regrouped. It is easier to group children in the skill development areas (language arts and mathematics) by the child's achievement level. There are various techniques in grouping children for skills as explained in Chapter Three.

It is desirable to regroup the children for the content areas, thus allowing different types of children to work and play together. Various techniques for grouping children in the content subjects was also explained in Chapter Three.

In organizing for instructional groups in the nongraded school, teachers, children, and parents should be involved in the grouping plans and all should be informed when a child is moved to another group, phase, or level within the nongraded program.

ROLE OF THE TEACHER

The teacher of the modern nongraded school will be expected to make his understanding of the cognitive process and skill development operational in his plans for instruction.

Since each teacher is personally different in his learning style, he will be as different in his teaching style. Recent research provides evidence that learning is an exceedingly complex personalized process, not only because of the differences in the learner himself, but also because learning is an expression of the entire person. Therefore, learning experiences must be provided for the learner which are personalized between the child's abilities and his personal characteristics. Furthermore, once knowing these factors concerning the child, and realizing that growth is continuous a close relationship is needed to help each child evaluate and select his next personalized and appropriate experience.

In planning the curriculum in the nongraded school, the teacher must be a "learning diagnostician" if he is to determine the conceptual schemes operating within the student and to determine when he is ready for a new and challenging experience.

The teacher is also a resource person for an individual or a group of children. Therefore, he must be aware of the many resources,

THE CURRICULUM

materials, and media available to help the student have his next confrontation or make his next discovery. He also uses talents to bring the resources and students together. In other words, he helps the child find his answers.

Another aspect of the teacher-learner relationship in the flexible school is that the student is able to freely develop his choices. The opportunity to develop full choices and the protection of this right for each child becomes the responsibility of the teacher in the nongraded school. The aim of the staff in the nongraded school is to create the kind of situation in which the child can create, plan, discover, and experiment.

It is essential that the teacher know how to develop learning behavioral objectives since much of the work is self-directed and self-evaluated in the nongraded learning environment. The teacher will spend more time in evaluating how well the pupils have accomplished the objectives in the content in the predetermined sequence at each level or phase of the continued progress.

The teacher should also provide experiences in which the child is allowed to play and work with different types of children. Here the teacher and children can appreciate their differences and respect their backgrounds. Therefore, the teaching staff of the nongraded school will see that no child will remain in any one grouping situation for even a day.

Above all, the teacher of the nongraded school will not only respect the differences of children but will learn to respect the differences of staff members and work together cooperatively to accomplish the best for all involved in the program.

SUMMARY

In summary, Chapter Five stressed the significance of professional objectives for curriculum planners; gave some considerations of what to teach; explained how the content should be taught; pointed out that subject matter divisions could be artificial if established merely for convenience; showed how scope and sequence should be considered for developing continuous progress; stressed that in organizing for instruction, flexibility is essential; and discussed the unique role of the teacher in the nongraded school.

*Those who educate children well are
more to be honored than even their
parents.*

6

Aristotle

Utilization of Staff:
A Team Approach for Planning

COOPERATIVE PLANNING

It is obvious that if nongraded programs succeed, cooperative planning is required from the complete staff. If the total staff does not understand the purpose of the nongraded plan and accept the basic goals of nongradedness, and plan cooperatively toward these goals, one cannot expect the program to be a success.

It is imperative that the principal develop a plan for working with a team of teachers in a cooperative manner. The plan should be flexible enough to permit the team to deal with problems as they arise in the nongraded structure.

Planning sessions are essential to success and they should be regularly scheduled. During these planning sessions the staff is encouraged and stimulated by colleagues; they become more enthusiastic. A successful nongraded team teaching program depends more upon people than other factors.

Some of the important problems encountered in the nongraded

UTILIZATION OF STAFF

team teaching program which can be discussed during planning sessions, thus adding to the security and effectiveness of the program, are:

1. How shall we use aides and interns in the program?
2. How will the space be utilized?
3. Who will work in large groups, small groups, and with individuals?
4. What kind of material will be needed; who shall produce or collect the media?
5. What units of work should be written?
6. Who will contact the resource people?
7. Who will arrange the large area or small areas for instructional purposes?
8. How will the team schedule time for planning?

These planning sessions serve as a mutual exchange of information among the principal, team teachers, aides, student teachers, specialists, and others who are assigned to the team.

The principal and instructional consultants may assume the leadership of the planning sessions if needed in the beginning stages of the planning periods. After several meetings they begin playing a minor role as the teachers themselves accept the responsibility for leadership.

Each team within the nongraded program meets at the time most convenient for them. These meetings focus on different but related aspects of the overall program for a certain group of children. Sometimes teams of the same content areas meet separately, while other times interdisciplinary teams meet to accomplish their goals.

For example, a team, whether it be a content team or an interdisciplinary team, may meet for planning in the nongraded school for the following reasons:

Meeting One: Organization of team operation with the principal.
Meeting Two: Identifying children for grouping purposes with the help of the guidance counselor.

Meeting Three: Placing children in appropriate grouping and regrouping situations.

Meeting Four: Selecting appropriate material for certain groups of children by the aide of the instructional supervisor.

Meeting Five: Focus on facilities and instructional methods.

Meeting Six: How to present a large group instruction lesson.

The chapter on team teaching explained that long and short range planning should be an essential ingredient for effective nongraded programs.

THE PRINCIPAL'S ROLE

The principal's primary role is that of providing instructional leadership, then comes his responsibility for building management and public relations. The principal either prohibits or encourages change. His support is expected if the staff changes.

When instructional change is concerned, as it is in the nongraded school, there is no substitute for a principal who knows children, instruction, and how to work with people. Nearly every nongraded team teaching program that experienced success had the principals closely connected with its implementation.

The big concern in all of this is proper coordination. As teams of teachers, aides, and interns pursue worthy but uncoordinated goals, they tend to produce confusion within the nongraded program. Sometimes the planned programs fail unless the principal is in the "doing and acting." The principal must provide the leadership for unification of efforts on the part of these teams at work in the nongraded school. If he is unable to coordinate these efforts he should appoint a coordinator of learning activities.

The principal's involvement means more than "just talk" and formulating objectives. Involvement should mean cutting across the teams of teachers, specialists, aides, students, parents, and other people who are likely to be affected.

These changes in the principal's role create a variety of concerns for those who work in the nongraded program. These major concerns are: (1) how to help team members develop skills and attitudes necessary for carrying out their new roles; (2) how to help teachers keep pace with new methods, materials, and content; (3) how to inform teachers on new organizational approaches; (4) ways of reporting progress to parents and children; and (5) how to help teachers in providing more effective learning situations for children.

He should be active in helping teacher teams and guidance counselors analyze problems and to consider alternatives to solve them. In short, he will serve as a learning counselor as well as a coordinator of the different teams at work in the nongraded program.

TEACHER SELECTION

Naturally, new programs and organizational patterns will be implemented more successfully if building principals are provided with the opportunity to interview and select candidates for teaching positions in their school. It is readily acknowledged that the principal will have a greater understanding of the position to be filled and the qualifications a prospective teacher should possess.

As schools establish programs designed to most effectively utilize their facilities and teachers' talents they will have a need for many different types of teachers and teaching styles. For example, a school which is moving toward individualization through team teaching will seek a teacher skilled in a major subject area such as science to lead the teaching team. Another school which seeks to establish a new organizational pattern following a year of intensive planning will want to employ teachers who are interested in innovation, willing to spend extra time working out a new program and planning to remain at the school more than one year.

In many instances it would be most beneficial to provide opportunities for teachers to interview prospective teachers. When a faculty chooses to utilize cooperative planning it would be vital for the teachers to have a cohesive group capable of learning and planning together.

The idea of a central office personnel director employing teachers and assigning them to a specific school is clearly detrimental to the best interests of most school programs. The personnel director must begin to establish his role as an individual who attracts qualified applicants to the school district and channels them to schools within the district for intensive personnel interviews. This will bring us one step closer to placing teachers in positions where they will be productive and satisfied, thus enhancing the total school program.

TEACHER'S RESPONSIBILITIES

As teachers plan cooperatively it is important that they see themselves as they are; know that what takes place in the planning for children must take place through interaction with team members and children. They must realize that "skills" to be worthwhile for the child must be functional in his life; and that human relations and values should be included as they plan the educational experiences of children.

In essence, the teacher's responsibility in planning involves working with people in effecting change. To accomplish this objective the following basic considerations should be a vital part of their planning period.

1. Organizes the learning experiences in some logical and usable form.

2. Understands the group process skills.

3. Knows that the communication skills are important.

4. Understands that insight into the psychological factors involved in changing human behavior is important.

5. Knows that technical skills essential for program development should be understood.

6. Understands that both theory and research in curriculum development is essential.

7. Knows to include each member in the planning and implementation of the program.

Planning time, well-used, promises more time for the teacher to work with the individuals in the nongraded situation. During the planning periods more information about students should be an important task of the planning team. Appropriate use of aides and student teachers may give the teacher more time to prepare work more effectively, e.g., T.V. viewing, listening to tapes, video tapes, and "micro-teaching."

These experiences can be accomplished through the division of responsibilities of the teaching team. For a team to be effective it must have a leader. The role of the team leader and teaching team was explained in the chapter on team teaching.

USING SPECIALISTS

The success of the specialists in the nongraded program can only be measured by the duties clearly specified by the planning team in which they are members. Specialists must know what is expected of them in the nongraded program; team members must also know the specialists' role on the team. Coordination of efforts is essential if time, energy, and the content presented are to be effective.

Guidance Counselor

The guidance counselor is a very important person on the teaching team. He not only gives and interprets tests but he helps schedule the children in proper content areas. He helps to evaluate the child's progress and advises him concerning his next educational experience. The guidance counselor also helps the teaching team develop behavioral objectives which should be personally prescribed for each child according to his needs.

Physical Education

Physical education teachers are not only members of the planning team in the nongraded school especially where they must be concerned about (1) health problems, (2) the development of posture, (3) proper grooming, and good nutrition. They are effective in large group and small group presentations. In many schools the physical education specialist with the help of an aide takes a large group of children in his education class while the rest of the team members plan.

The Arts

In the social studies content areas of the nongraded school, where social living is stressed, music and art help concepts become more meaningful to children. Here the arts are correlated with the content bringing the areas studied to life and motivating the children to want to learn. The arts specialists are very worthwhile members of the team in helping in large group situations by correlating the arts with the content to be presented.

Foreign Language

The foreign language specialist is also helpful in the nongraded school. Foreign language can be used as a means of helping to make social studies meaningful to children. The foreign language teacher also helps in large group situations when relating the language with the country being studied. Foreign language can also be an excellent means for enriching the learning experiences of small groups of children.

The chart on page 141 depicts how the specialists are scheduled for the teams at Cresent Elementary Nongraded School, Greenville, Tennessee.

ROLE AND DUTIES OF TEACHER AIDES

The needs of society require significant changes in our present school organization. The teacher is no longer a person who teaches and expects the children to learn. The teacher is a skilled professional and should be permitted to do a professional level of work. He must be a diagnostician and a planner of learning experiences. He should not waste his time on non-professional tasks. The utilization of auxiliary personnel can provide the opportunity for teachers to devote their time to the best advantage of the child.

Auxiliary personnel are here to stay, and they are here because they are needed, especially where educators are attempting to individualize instruction.

Supporting this argument, Senate Bill 721, termed Teacher Aid Program Support Act of 1967 and prepared by Robert Gilberts, Superintendent of the Madison, Wisconsin School System, was introduced in the First Session of the 90th Congress by Gaylord Nelson, United States Senator from Wisconsin. At the time the bill was introduced, Senator Nelson commented that:

> ... the proposed legislation would be a major step toward relieving the burden of the elementary and secondary classroom teacher through the utilization of teacher aides—personnel qualified to perform clerical and monitorial tasks now required of teachers and, under the supervision of certified teachers, to assist children in need of additional instruction and attention.[1]

---

[1] "S. 721 Teacher Aid Program Support Act of 1967," *The National Elementary Principal*, XLVI (May,1967), p. 40.

UTILIZATION OF STAFF

Crescent ELEMENTARY SCHOOL PROGRAM
SPECIAL TEACHERS SCHEDULE

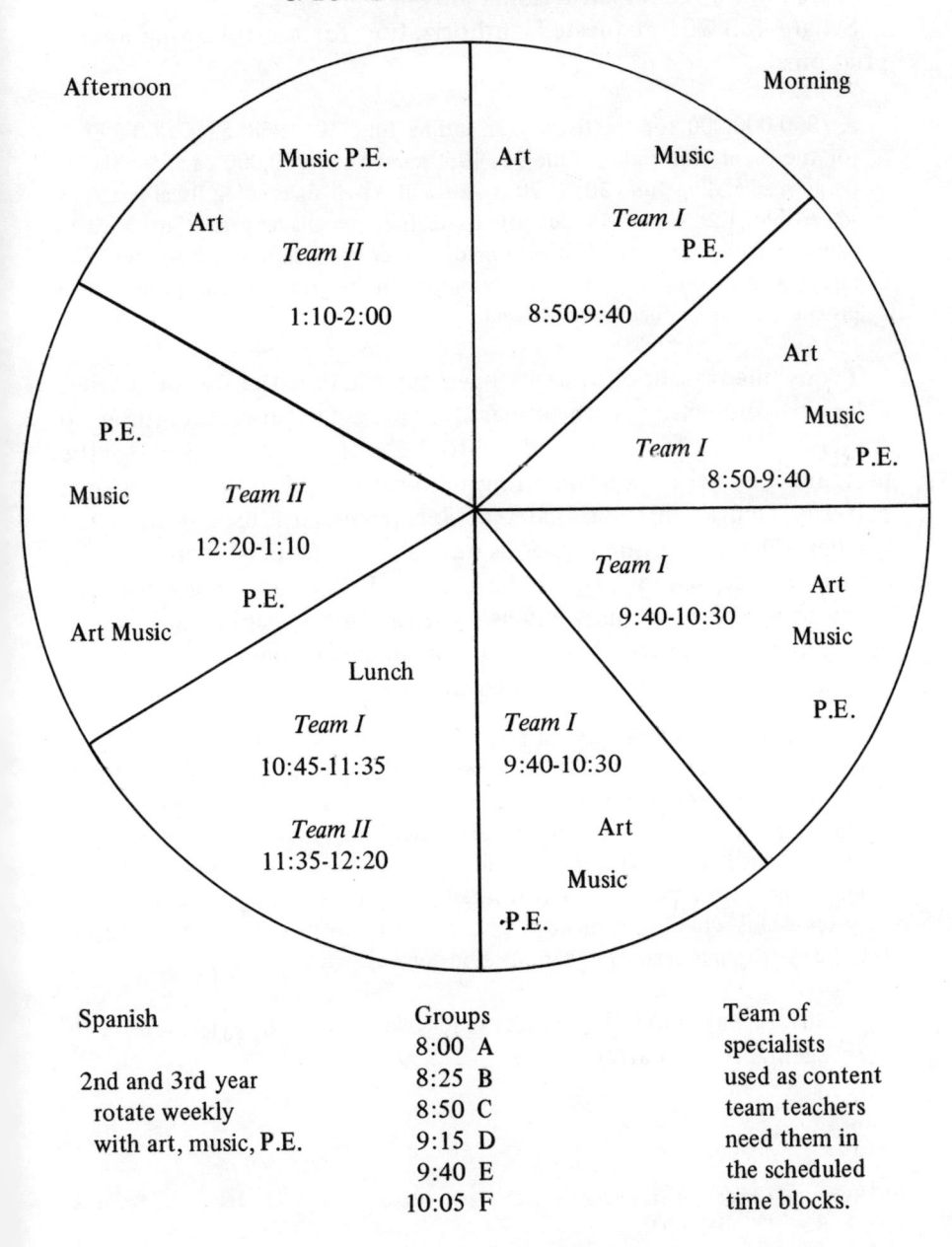

Afternoon

Morning

Music P.E.

Art

Music

Art

Team I
P.E.

Team II

1:10-2:00

8:50-9:40

Art

P.E.

Music

Music

Team I
P.E.

Team I

8:50-9:40

Team II

12:20-1:10

Art

P.E.

Team I

Art

Art Music

9:40-10:30

Music

Lunch

P.E.

Team I

Team I

10:45-11:35

9:40-10:30

Team II

Art

11:35-12:20

Music

·P.E.

Spanish

2nd and 3rd year
rotate weekly
with art, music, P.E.

Groups
8:00 A
8:25 B
8:50 C
9:15 D
9:40 E
10:05 F

Team of
specialists
used as content
team teachers
need them in
the scheduled
time blocks.

Nelson further stated that "a study made several years ago revealed that from 21 per cent to 69 per cent of a teacher's day is occupied by . . . non-instructional jobs."[2]

Senate Bill 721 requested authorization for the following appropriations:

> . . . $50,000,000 for the fiscal year ending June 30, 1968, $100,000,000 for the fiscal year ending June 30, 1969, and $150,000,000 each for the fiscal year ending June 30, 1970, and for the two succeeding fiscal years, to enable the Commissioner of Education to make grants to local educational agencies and institutions of higher education to assist them in carrying out projects for the development of teacher aid programs provided for in application approved under this Act.[3]

Today many school systems have experienced the use of teacher aides in connection with nongraded programs and, according to Anderson, have found the aides to be a tremendous asset to the program.[4] Systems experimenting with various school organizational patterns such as instructional teaching teams have usually included teacher aides who assume various duties as members of their assigned teams. In fact, school systems have viewed this team arrangement as a way to incorporate merit pay as duties and responsibilities are more differentiated than with traditional teaching assignments.

Charles S. Benson's comment to this possibility is:

> It is apparent that the plan of merit would hold under a policy including instructional teams and hence differentiated salary policy, as well as under the existing prevalent monolithic staff and salary schedule policies. However, it might be that differentiated staffs and corresponding differentiated pay schedules would be highly beneficial toward the recruitment of more competent workers in the classrooms of local school systems and would also make it possible in terms of economics to pay more appropriate salaries to various kinds of workers.[5]

Factors concerning the widespread use of auxiliary personnel in new organizational patterns are:

---

[2] *Ibid*, p. 44.

[3] *Ibid*, p. 42.

[4] Robert H. Anderson, *Teaching in a Changing World*. (New York: Harcourt, Brace & World, Inc., 1966), p. 119.

[5] Charles S. Benson. *Perspectives on the Economics of Education*. (Boston: Houghton Mifflin Company, 1963), p. 405.

UTILIZATION OF STAFF

1. The extending curriculum, and the concept of differentiated roles for teachers such as flexible scheduling, cooperative team teaching, and different approaches to learning require more and varied personnel.

2. Demands for school services in the nongraded schools, including the use of different materials, checking of skill sheets, conferences with parents, use of different audio-visual aides and technology requires much time, "know-how" and energy.

3. An awareness of the special learning needs of the disadvantaged, and the availability of federal funds for employing them have encouraged nongraded schools to use the auxiliary personnel for individualizing instruction.

Generally, the effective use of teacher aides should be determined by capitalizing on the special talents of the aides.

In the case of teacher aides, they will not initiate learning activities unless directed by the teacher. Neither will they make professional judgments related to a diagnosis of students' skill level or needs. They may perform in certain drill or reinforcing activities or in various clerical functions. They may work with children in any general capacity, e.g., tutoring, independent study, or in a seminar; they should not direct the learning process. As team members, they will plan with the teachers and help decide what their assignments should be. In these essential activities, they can be of invaluable help in furthering the program of instruction.

In the nongraded team teaching situation some aides devote their time primarily or exclusively to clerical tasks, while other aides perform the tasks involving the children; others are classified as audio-visual aides.

A clerical aide is usually assigned to a nongraded unit or to a team teaching staff. Most of her duties are performed on paper. The teacher aide works closely with the teacher and children. She plans with the team and helps support their plans by preparing materials, working with the children on individual work on routine operations. The materials aide helps prepare transparencies, makes charts, gets out the audio-visual equipment, and runs the machine for the teachers. She also aids the children at viewing and listening stations by helping them with tapes, recordings, filmstrips, earphones, and at the dial access.

Following are some "do's and don'ts" for teacher aides as they work as team members in the nongraded program.

DO'S AND DON'TS FOR TEACHER AIDES

DO

1. Attend faculty meetings and in-service education programs on the nongraded program.

2. Help promote good public relations.

3. Help your team members build good public relations.

4. Do such a good job in your work that you will help team members build good public relations.

5. Remember that children have differences, too.

6. Give the best of yourself to the girls and boys with whom you work.

DON'T

1. Be guilty of comparing one pupil with another at any time.

2. Make unfair remarks about lead teachers, team members, supervisors, and other administrative personnel.

3. Complain about the duties you have as a team member.

4. Refer to pupils in such a manner as to indicate your dislike or disapproval.

5. Wait to be told everything to do; use your own initiative to make the program successful.

6. Talk about the nongraded program "outside of school," unless you understand the philosophy.

Teacher aides like all other staff members should present a favorable image of the nongraded school. Therefore, it is very important for the teacher aide to be knowledgeable enough to talk intelligently about the nongraded school organization. The following suggestions should be discussed with the aides in explaining their role in helping to give the program a favorable image with the public.

TEACHER AIDES AND PUBLIC RELATIONS

1. The teacher aide should present to the public a favorable image of the nongraded school.

2. Questions asked by the parents or others outside the school concerning the nongraded program should be answered only with positive statements. No attempt should be made to evaluate students. Refer the person to the teacher or the principal.

UTILIZATION OF STAFF

3. The teacher aide will have good public relations if he and/or she is tactful and courteous with parents.

4. When new pupils come into the room, help the teacher give them and their parent and/or parents a warm welcome.

5. The teacher aide should recognize his and/or her position on the "team," developing respect for team relationships in the learning process.

6. The teacher aide should be an active member of the P.T.A. and other school parent-teacher groups.

As stated before, teacher-teacher aide relations are essential in a nongraded program where cooperative planning is imperative for effective programs. The following concerns should be considered as teachers and teacher aides plan cooperatively:

TEACHER—TEACHER AIDE RELATIONS

1. The teacher aide will not replace the certified teacher as instructor—the responsibilities are many and contributions valuable which the aide may make; he and/or she will be a supporting member of a team.

2. Both teacher and teacher aide should understand their job description in the nongraded program.

3. The teacher and teacher aide should understand their jobs and be familiar with plans and procedures of the regular day as well as long range planning.

4. Both the teacher and teacher aide should accept the limitations placed upon the aide as an assistant to the trained professional.

5. When questions or problems concerning children present themselves in the nongraded program, discuss these first of all with the teacher. If the problem is of major significance where the welfare of the child is jeopardized, go to the person next in authority.

6. The practice of keeping confidence with team members will strengthen and maintain the confidence of the regular classroom team.

7. The lead teacher and team teachers have the responsibility for planning,

instructing, and evaluating. All major decisions concerning classroom management and discipline will be their professional responsibility. The teacher aide's suggestions and council may be useful in helping the team effect the objectives desired. If the aide does not agree with the team on procedures or decisions made, in the final analysis, the decision is in the hands of the lead teacher, team teachers or principal.

The kinds of jobs and responsibilities of auxiliary personnel can vary greatly and are influenced by their educational philosophy, instructional level, kind of community, and other factors. In using auxiliary personnel in the nongraded program a few major job categories are evident and suggest the scope of possible paraprofessional tasks.

The following tasks for elementary auxiliary persons in the nongraded school are:

1. Supervising the playground and lunchroom giving teacher teams time for planning.

2. Preparing audio-visual aids for large and small group institutions.

3. Making masters for skill sheets and other numerous forms needed in the nongraded programs.

4. Recording tests and grades on progression skill sheets.

5. Making summaries of teacher team planning.

6. Taking inventory of materials for use in divisions or groups.

7. Reading to small groups of children.

8. Listening to children in small groups.

9. Acting as a resource person in the materials and resource center.

10. Playing the piano and other instruments for large group instruction.

11. Helping to order instructional materials and audio-visual equipment.

12. Typing personal letters and newsletters to parents.

13. Arranging conferences with parents and teachers.

UTILIZATION OF STAFF

14. Delivering materials to small groups and individuals.

15. Collecting money, taking attendance, and supervising the bus duties.

16. Tutoring in remedial reading.

17. Filing, circulating, and clipping pictures.

18. Typing units for long range planning.

19. Helping with the creative arts.

20. Assisting in large groups, small groups, and individual instruction.

21. Helping check individual papers.

The following are activities which have been identified as being successfully performed by auxiliary personnel in the team teaching situations:

1. Gets and puts away instructional materials required by the teacher.

2. Corrects papers.

3. Supervises independent pupil study.

4. Makes entries on pupil's progress chart.

5. Supervises children while teachers plan.

6. Operates the projector.

7. Types the plans for the team.

8. Takes part in discussion groups.

9. Is a leader in seminars.

10. Arranges the room for large group instruction.

11. Calls homes of pupil absentees to determine reason for absence.

12. Makes routine announcements.

13. Supervises pupils during lunch.

14. Receives requests for supplies.

15. Types letters, worksheets, and tests.

16. Helps the librarian collect the material for small group discussions and independent study.

17. Tutors children needing help.

18. Helps in large group presentations.

In viewing the many and varied ways teacher aides can be utilized in the flexible school program as shown in this section, auxiliary personnel can be a tremendous asset to the teaching/learning process. They can enhance better staff utilization practices; they can boost the professionalization and image of the teacher; and, the additional auxiliary personnel can help facilitate changes in both curriculum and school organizational practices. These services ultimately should improve the quality of the educational unit.

SELECTION OF TEACHER AIDES

The first step in selecting aides for nongraded school programs should be to select people who seem capable of being effective helpers with children. The second consideration should take into account their willingness to work in a flexible school program; they should also consent to enter an in-service program to understand the nongraded school organization.

Each aide should be interviewed before he is accepted to work in a nongraded team teaching situation. In the initial interview the principal should attempt to gauge the individual's motivations, assess his potential contributions, and decide the responsibility he may effectively assume in the nongraded program.

It is difficult to specify qualifications until the requirements of particular jobs are determined, and they are in turn influenced by the manpower pool available. Decisions about qualifications should depend upon the services rendered in the nongraded program.

Basic Requirements

Certain items are requisites for all candidates. The following list represents the basic requirements of all teaching aides whether they are in a nongraded school or in a traditional classroom:

1. Pleasing personality
2. Educational background
3. Poise and appearance
4. Likes children
5. Past employment
6. General health
7. English usage
8. Evidence of good mental health

The interview will also serve to inform the aide of the philosophy of the nongraded program, how the program is organized, and how he and/or she will function in the program. At this time the aide should be told also that he and/or she should engage in an extensive in-service program on the nongraded team teaching approach. This training should depend upon the job for which the aide is being prepared and the educational levels which have been attained.

Special Talents and Skills

Some very special skills like the following provide added dividends for the aides working in a nongraded team teaching school:

1. Able to play the piano
2. Artistic: painting and crafts.
3. Dancing and rhythm talents
4. Storytelling and dramatics
5. Corrective reading experience
6. Composition ability
7. Playwriter
8. Newspaper experience
9. Photography
10. Scientific knowledge

The special talents and skills enable the aide to assist in small groups and help the team members with special talented children. They can also tutor children from homes of limited economic backgrounds in helping to build a good self-image.

Ethics of the Profession

Since more information of a diagnostic nature is essential for the child in a nongraded program, something should be done during the interview to sensitize the aide to the ethics of the profession. There should also be some policies and procedures written down for the protection of the program, and methods for enforcing them should be clear.

Volunteer Aide

There is no adequate way to reward a conscientious volunteer aide for the services which he and/or she shall render in a nongraded program, e.g., helping with field trips, repairing audio-visual equipment, helping children collect material for independent study, making slides, contacting community resources, and helping to check papers.

These volunteer parent aides should be selected by the principal and team members since they are to work with them directly. It is imperative that they, too, understand the philosophy of the nongraded program and have the qualifications to operate effectively in the program. It is also essential that parents from different social ethnic and economic backgrounds be selected in order that all children may have someone in the school they can identify with easily.

On page 151 the application blank for a position as an aide helps the administrator evaluate the aide as a potential employee.

IN-SERVICE PROGRAM FOR TOTAL STAFF

In order for the personnel to play an effective role in the nongraded school, a whole plan of training is required: a continuous training system. The system should begin with (1) administrative planning and the recruitment and selection of appropriate staff; (2) the involvement of the staff in the planning; (3) pre- and in-service training for the principal, team members, specialists, interns, aides, and all other personnel who will work with the program; and (4) the in-service should be continuous.

The in-service training should be concerned not only with the cognitive dimensions, but also with the attitudinal elements involved in the development of an effective nongraded program. Special

UTILIZATION OF STAFF   151

APPLICATION FOR POSITION AS AIDE

Interview Date:_____

By Whom: _____

For:_____

Remarks:_____

Name:_____
    Last   First   Middle

Address_____

Phone No._____ Social Security No._____

Date of Birth:_____ _____ _____
     year   month   day

U.S. Citizen _____yes? _____no?

Married_____ Single_____

General Health: Excellent_____ Good_____ Fair_____ Poor_____

Have you ever worked with children? If so, where_____
_____

Why did you decide to be an aide?_____
_____

What are your special talents?_____
_____
_____

Check what you can do well:

Typing_____ Clerk_____ File Clerk_____
Library work_____ Machines_____ Bookkeeping_____
Art_____ Receptionist____ Dancing_____
Sewing_____ Music_____ Tutoring_____

APPLICATION FOR
POSITION AS AIDE (cont.)

Education:

Grade School attended _____
                      Name   Where   When

High School _____
                      Name   Where   When

College _____
                      Name   Where   When

Business School _____
                      Name   Where   When

Vocational _____
                      Name   Where   When

Work Experience:

      Date: Firm: Position:

1. _____

2. _____

3. _____

4. _____

Reference:

Vocational: _____
_____
_____

Character: _____
_____
_____

                                        Signed _____

                                        Date _____

UTILIZATION OF STAFF

in-service for the staff cannot be overemphasized. Without adequate in-service, a nongraded plan is not possible. So many people plan "just enough to fail" and then say it does not work.

An effective in-service program should include the following experiences:

1. Read the literature concerning "well-known" nongraded programs.

2. Study the related literature on grouping.

3. Visit "well-known" nongraded programs.

4. Attend college classes on "Newer Trends in Education."

5. Study the school to see how it might be nongraded to meet the needs of the children.

6. Have outstanding consultants discuss how the school might be nongraded.

7. Study how the school might utilize the staff effectively: team members, teacher aides, interns, volunteer aides, and specialists.

8. Examine different organizational patterns.

9. Study how teams plan: long and short range planning.

10. Discuss reporting progress in the nongraded school.

11. Acquaint the staff with public relation techniques.

12. Discuss how the nongraded school might be evaluated.

The in-service program for implementing nongraded programs should be directed toward achieving at least the following objectives:

1. It should be closely related to the objectives of the nongraded program.

2. It should fully involve the learners in the learning process.

3. It should be closely related to the actual job experience.

4. It should be custom-designed to meet the total staff's particular training needs.

5. It should be interesting enough to motivate the learner to learn.

6. It should involve work on a long-range and short-range basis.

7. It should bring about effective behavior as well as efficient skills.

8. A "follow-up" program should accompany the staff for security and encouragement; the trainee should see his success while implementing this program.

The specific techniques to be used in the in-service program should derive from several primary considerations; e.g., discussions, job-related activities, real task—down-to-earth style, lectures from consultants, and use of modern media.

In-service techniques with broad implications for nongraded programs as well as teacher skills should be used. The following laboratory techniques are effective:

Role Playing

In this procedure the participants are given an opportunity to take the role or roles they will play in the nongraded team teaching situation. Role reversals are also effective when the staff members see a relationship from the "other person's" point of view.

In-Basket

This technique "spells out" problem situations; the group with the aid of the information at hand decides how best to solve the problems presented.

Job Simulation

In this process a series of incidents are created. In a sense, the staff sees an entire play of what is happening in the nongraded team teaching situation on whatever is studied. These incidents are portrayed through written incidents, films, tapes, and other sources. The information available helps a group come up with some kind of a solution after much study, discussion, and observation.

Video-Tapes

Actual observation of ones behavior on the teaching team or working individually as a team member can be revealed through the video-tape recording of one's actual self in action. Here one can see how he reacts in a group and how his behavior can be modified as he observes himself in action.

Inter-group Reaction

This an excellent technique for team members to use in trying to understand how to relate to each other in a team teaching situation. As the staff discusses important issues involved in nongraded programs they take turns as group members, recorders, and leaders, thus, allowing the staff to study the behavior of each member.

A comprehensive in-service plan for in-servicing teachers who were to work in a nongraded program in Abingdon, Virginia was presented in Chapter One.

The following pre-service program was held for new aides who were to work in two nongraded schools in Wise County, Virginia. This pre-service program was conducted by the curriculum director of the Dilenowisco Educational Cooperative Center and funded by the Educational Professional Developmental Act. Continuous in-service experiences were planned for the aides throughout the year including the team teachers and student teachers, e.g., visitations to exemplary innovative programs, college classes, seminars, and personal classroom help.

The outline of the workshop for the aides who were to work in nongraded team teaching situations follows:

IN—SERVICE WORKSHOP FOR ELEMENTARY SCHOOL AIDES AND OTHER AUXILIARY PERSONNEL

I. Objectives of Teacher Aide and Other Auxiliary Personnel

    A. Maximum assistance for students
    B. Provide proper supervision of students
    C. Effective use of personnel
    D. Provide time for teachers to perform professional duties

II. Qualifications

    A. Education
    B. Character
    C. Ability and talents
    D. Availability to the school
    E. Experience working with children
    F. Health and emotional stability

III. Duties and Services

    A. Help students with special problems
    B. Supervise study periods and lunch programs
    C. Take attendance and keep records
    D. Make bulletin board displays
    E. Work with audio-visual aides
    F. Help tutor children
    G. Check papers of children
    H. Assist with bus duties
    I. Assist with special subjects where talents are needed—(art, music, drama)
    J. Type seatwork, lesson plans, and tests for teacher
    K. Making transparencies
    L. Ordering and returning films
    M. Helping children who were absent from school
    N. Assisting with independent study

IV. The Role of Aides and Other Auxiliary Personnel in Staff Utilization

    A. Scheduling
    B. Team planning
    C. Team teaching
    D. Working with facilities
    E. Evaluating

V. Working with Children

    A. Basic needs of children
    B. Discipline
    C. Understanding behavioral problems
    D. How to work in small groups
    E. How to work individually

UTILIZATION OF STAFF

VI. Working with Parents

    A. P.T.A. meetings
    B. Informal conversations
    C. Working with parents in informal situations
    D. Helping parents with field trips

VII. Practical Implications: How It Is Done? How Do I Do What I Am Expected To Do?

    (The following taught through demonstrations, laboratory techniques, films, filmstrips, lectures, visitations, and role playing)

    1. How to make the classroom attractive

        a. Bulletin boards
        b. Seating arrangements
        c. Pictures, charts, etc.

    2. How to help prepare materials

        a. Mimeograph work
        b. Charts, models, pictures
        c. Prepare equipment, art, science, music, etc.
        d. Felt board, etc.
        e. Make transparencies

    3. Audio-visual aide

        a. How to operate film projectors, filmstrip projectors, record players, and tape recorders

    4. Record keeping
        a. Attendance records
        b. Lunch records
        c. Other record keeping, special activities, routine matters

    5. Games for physical education

        a. Races, drills
        b. Circle games

  c. Dances and rhythms
  d. Ball games

6. Story telling and rhymes
  a. How to tell a story
  b. Dramatize a story
  c. Finger games for children
  d. Use of puppets

7. Drills for helping individual children

  a. Use of programmed material
  b. Drill cards, games, devices, etc.
  c. Workbooks and skill sheets
  d. Teaching machines

8. How to work in the library

  a. Use of card catalogue
  b. How to find materials
  c. How to mend the library books
  d. Arrange materials

9. Field trips

  a. How to organize field trips
  b. Arranging for the field trip, parents, children, resource persons, etc.

COMMUNITY RESOURCES

 When planning for the nongraded team teaching approach, the staff should consider what lifelike projects are in the community. The staff must ask: "Are the time and energy involved in this project worth the benefits the children will receive?"

 It is also essential to look beyond the benefits that the children will receive from the surface appearance. In the process, we should work toward other objectives, e.g., working and sharing with others, speaking and listening in a group situation, drawing and painting what one observed, and creating stories, poems, and music from the experience. Many times the staff may plan functional experiences which involve the children in the activity.

 These trips to the community should be planned with all team

UTILIZATION OF STAFF

members so that they do not interfere with other groups in the nongraded school.

Some basic considerations in planning field trips are:

1. The trip should supplement the learning experiences in the classroom.

2. The team members should acquaint the children: (1) with the place they plan to visit, (2) what they are expected to learn on the trip, and (3) with the principal as to why they are going.

3. The team members should ask the children to make a list of questions that they wish to have answered a day before the trip.

4. Following the trip, there should be a follow-up discussion; the list could guide the discussion.

5. There should be permission slips signed by the parents of each child taking the trip.

6. Teacher aides and volunteer parent-aides serve as excellent "helpers" for field trips.

Resource persons are also a vital part of the teaching team. They, too, should be informed beforehand what the class will want to know. If not, the visit will be less profitable than it might have been. It must be remembered that a resource person without the help of the team does not know what phases of his work will be of most interest to the group.

In addition, the team leader should inform the resource person on what he is to say, questions the group plans to ask, and what materials to bring for display.

SUMMARY

This chapter stressed the value of cooperative planning in the nongraded team teaching school. As stated before, it is imperative that the total staff plan the learning experiences of the children to insure continuity. Effective utilization of *all* staff members, specialists, and resource persons is essential if the children are to derive the benefits of the talents of the total staff. Aides and other auxiliary personnel are vital members of any teaching team when they are functioning effectively. In-service education on the nongraded school is imperative for all who are concerned with the nongraded school program; the principal is the key person in the total process.

7

Every mind is different; and the more it is unfolded, the more pronounced is that difference.

Emerson, *Essay on Quotations and Originality*

A Look at Reporting Practices: Continuous Evaluation of the Individual Pupil

The importance of maintaining accurate and up-to-date records for the nongraded elementary school cannot be overemphasized. Since children will function in flexible grouping situations allowing for individual differences, a thorough system of reporting should complement the plan. Adequate records and reporting help children and their parents to understand themselves better. Through comprehensive evaluation techniques, the child should be helped to discover himself and his potential, without regard to arbitrary standards. Teachers, parents, and consultants should collaborate in the nongraded school to evaluate the child according to his own unique, individual growth pattern.

A LOOK AT REPORTING PRACTICES

ESSENTIAL RECORDS

The cumulative record is the most widely used means of recording information about every individual child. These essential records should immediately provide an abundance of accurate and complete information that can be studied from the developmental point of view. The following kinds of information should be recorded by the school system: (1) name, (2) age, (3) birthdate, (4) sex, (5) scholarship, (6) attendance, (7) health records, (8) standardized test scores, (9) personal characteristics, (10) student activities, (11) sociometric records, (12) anecdotal records, (13) interviews, (14) social history, (15) examples of child's work, (16) name of parents, (17) address, and (18) occupation.

PUPIL PLACEMENT INFORMATION

Pupil placement forms should denote the level of progress of the child as he advances through the different learning experiences or areas of content. The level of the experience should be recorded to insure proper placement and to prevent the duplication of learning experiences.

The chart on page 162 illustrates how children can be placed in levels for reading.

PERSONALIZED SKILL SHEETS

The skill sheet represents an important aspect of skill teaching and provides a formal record of skills learned. Beyond this, they also function as a type of lesson plan. They should be developed before teaching begins and used as "check sheets" to determine the rate of pupil progress through the sequence of skills and/or facts which make up the content of the units being taught. Skill sheets are an absolute necessity in the nongraded elementary school, since skills are the core of the program. Skill sheets should be discussed with parents during conferences and with children whenever desirable.

It is essential that the skills prescribed for the child should be those needed by him. When the child learns the prescribed skills needed for his phase or level of achievement he should progress to a higher level. Skills should be prescribed with behavorial aims in mind.

PUPIL PLACEMENT INFORMATION

Student's Name _____ Assigned to Level _____

Date _____ Age _____

Check student's level for beginning next school year.

Language Arts

(1) Readiness	(2) P. Primer	(3) Primer	(4) First	(5) Second	(6) Second2
_____	_____	_____	_____	_____	_____

(7) Third	(8) Third2	(9) Fourth	(10) Fifth	(11) Sixth	(12) Seventh
_____	_____	_____	_____	_____	_____

Mathematics

Level

(1) Readiness	(2) Primer	(3) First	(4) Second	(5) Third	(6) Fourth
_____	_____	_____	_____	_____	_____

(7) Fifth	(8) Sixth	(9) Seventh
_____	_____	_____

Science and Health

Sequential Experiences in Broad Units

Units Completed
1_____ 2_____ 3_____ 4_____ 5_____ etc.

Social Studies

Units Completed
1_____ 2_____ 3_____ 4_____ 5_____ 6_____ etc.

Please list any unusual characteristics of the pupil's which his next teacher should know. Physical handicaps_____Hearing_____Speaking_____Foreign Language_____Physical Education_____

Please use reverse side for comments pertinent to teacher evaluation of student for placement.

A LOOK AT REPORTING PRACTICES 163

PUPIL PLACEMENT
INFORMATION (cont.)

	Reading		Math		Science
ACHIEVEMENT TEST SCORES					
INTELLIGENCE TEST SCORES	Year 1	Year 2	Year 3	Year 4	Year 5
READING TEXTBOOK TEST SCORES					

In other words, skills should be meaningful and functional if they are to be retained and used effectively.

Changes in level placement should be made at any time during the year when they would seem to be in the best interest of the child. In most schools children of the same age grow up enough alike so that a great majority move along with their age mates. Although grouping and regrouping should be consistent with the needs of the children, the school should not be involved in a constant reshuffling due to a too-finely drawn concept of a continuous "best placement" policy. Class sections for the ensuing year should be planned before the end of the current year so that individual adjustments in group assignments and individual prescribed work can be made while the teacher's familiarity with individual cases is greater. Chronological age should be only one factor considered in placement. The other factors in placement, you will remember, were thoroughly discussed in Chapters Two and Three.

The chart on page 164 depicts a skill sheet for reading for level eight.

Skill sheets in mathematics are essential for self-evaluation by the student and reporting to parents as well as for placement and progression in a phase or level of achievement. The check sheet on pages 165-166 for level five illustrates the skills to be taught in that phase or level of development.

The skill sheets on pages 167-168 used in science denote the scientific concepts, attitudes, and experimental skills. Children

NULL SCHOOL
CHECK SHEET FOR READING

STUDENT _____ TEACHER _____ 19__

	Level 8	Satis-factory	Unsatis-factory	Comments
I.	Vocabulary			
	A. Recognizes basic sight words (Teacher edition)			
	B. Use of context			
	1. Oral			
	2. Printed			
	C. Word Meaning			
	1. Likeness & opposite			
II.	Word Analysis			
	A. Letter-sound associations			
	1. Silent letters			
	2. Blends			
	3. Consonant sound associations			
	4. Vowel sound associations			
	B. Phonograms or rhyming elements			
	C. Structural elements			
	1. Endings and prefixes			
	2. Recognizing root words			
	3. Compound words			
	4. Contractions			
	5. Forming plurals			
	6. Syllables			
	a. 3 rules for dividing words into syllables			
III.	Comprehension and listening skills			
	A. Reading information articles			
	B. Distinguishing between fact and fiction			
	C. Interprets use of commas and figures of speech			
	D. Drawing conclusions			
	E. Main idea			
	F. Detail			
	G. Sequence			
IV.	Appreciation and oral reading			
	A. Recognizes vivid language			
	B. Judges whether an author achieves his purposes			
	C. Reading poetry, plays & prose			
	D. Meaningful oral reading			

LEVEL   7   8   9
Student Progress _____
Normal Progress _____

A LOOK AT REPORTING PRACTICES

PUPIL'S CHECK SHEET FOR ARITHMETIC

LEVEL FIVE

NAME_____AGE_____TEACHER_____

DATE STARTED_____DATE COMPLETED_____

_____ I. Vocabulary
    ____A. Double-near double
    ____B. Dozen-half dozen
    ____C. Names of coins
    ____D. Points (in geometry)
    ____E. Quadrilateral
    ____F. Freezing degrees-temperature
    ____G. Thousand
    ____H. Two-digit numbers

_____ II. Numeration system
    ____A. One to one correspondence
    ____B. Using expanded notation
    ____C. Grouping ten one's to make one ten
    ____D. Grouping ten ten's to make one hundred

_____ III. Basic operations
    ____A. Addition
        ____1. Facts 13's, 14's, 15's, 16's, 17's, 18's
        ____2. Addition without carrying, two digit-three digits
        ____3. Addition with carrying two digit carrying to tens place
        ____4. Addition with carrying three digits-carrying tens place, hundreds place
        ____5. Column addition with carrying
    ____B. Subtraction
        ____1. Subtraction facts 11's & 12's
        ____2. Subtraction with borrowing-two digit borrowing from tens place
        ____3. Three digit borrowing from ten and/or hundreds place

PUPIL'S CHECK SHEET FOR ARITHMETIC (cont.)

   ____C. Multiplication of whole numbers
        ____1. 2's in multiplication
        ____2. 3's in multiplication
        ____3. Half of a number
        ____4. The inverse

   ____D. Division
        ____1. Dividing by 2

   ____E. Fractions
        ____1. Fractional parts
            a. 1/4 – 1/2

   ____F. Number lines
        ____1. Verifying number facts on a number line
        ____2. Vertical format (thermometer)
        ____3. Ruler
        ____4. Showing number sentences

_____ IV. Measurements
     ____A. Time, length, weight, groups, liquid measure, value.

_____ V. Sets
     ____A. Matching elements one to one correspondence
     ____B. Identifying elements in sets
     ____C. Concepts of pairs

_____ VI. Problem solving
     ____A. Number sentences
         ____1. Writing number sentences from picture problems
         ____2. Writing number sentences from verbal description

_____ VII. Geometry
     ____A. Recognizing geometric shapes
     ____B. Points and line segments
     ____C. Geometric construction

A LOOK AT REPORTING PRACTICES

CONTINUOUS PROGRESS CHECKLIST FOR SCIENCE

Name _____ Date _____

Progression Unit Ages 9-10 The Plant World	Science, Scientific Concept, Attitudes and Experimentation Skills	Evidence of Learning
Concepts:	Man uses plants for many purposes.	*Diagnostic Tests*
	Green plants contain chlorophyll and can make their own food.	Above average _____ Average _____ Below average _____
	Some plants are among the largest of all living things.	*Scientific Attitudes*
	Green plants make their own food in the presence of sunlight.	Wants to know
	All plants of the highest group of green plants have roots, stems, and leaves.	*Observes*
	Water enters plants through small hairs on the roots.	Yes _____ No _____
	Plants cannot survive for long without a water supply.	Sometimes _____
	In order to make food a green plant needs carbon dioxide from the air, water from the soil, and energy from the sun.	Yes _____ No _____ Sometimes _____
	Higher plants produce seeds.	
	The fruit of a plant forms from the flower.	Applies what is learned.
	The non-green plants include fungi, such as bacteria, molds, yeast mushrooms and smuts.	Yes _____ No _____ Sometimes _____

CONTINUOUS PROGRESS CHECKLIST FOR SCIENCE (con't.)

Progression Unit Ages 9-10 The Plant World	Science, Scientific Concept, Attitudes and Experimentation Skills	Evidence of Learning
Concepts: (continued)		
	Fungi do not have roots, stems, leaves or flowers.	
	The plants best suited for their environment are the ones most likely to survive.	
Experimentation Skills	Can use equipment well when experimenting.	*Can handle material*
	Can share equipment.	Poorly _____
	Can predict the outcome of an experiment.	Fair _____
	Knows how to follow directions.	Well _____
		Is precise
	Can question and identify the elements of science studied.	Yes _____ No _____ Sometimes _____
Scientific Attitudes	Wants to question, explore, observe, and invent.	
	Shows evidence of curiosity.	
	Sees the "use and value" of the aspects of science being studied.	
	Can use what he has learned in daily life.	
	Uses science to help change his environment.	

A LOOK AT REPORTING PRACTICES

progress through a sequence of units at their own rate of speed. The evidence of learning is determined by tests, observation of scientific skills, and how the student applies what he learns.

The chart on pages 170-171 depicts the continuous progress check sheet for a social studies unit. This check list illustrates a progression unit for children, in age groups seven and eight, studying "Families and Their Needs." Skills checked for this unit are concepts, social skills, and study skills.

Evidence of learning these skills is evaluated by diagnostic tests, pupil self-evaluation, and teacher-pupil evaluation through observation of action and attitudes of the child.

As has been shown skill sheets can be effectively developed for all areas of the curriculum. The sample skill sheets in this chapter and in the appendix provide a model for teachers and schools as they develop skill sheets consistent with the needs of their children.

The variety of ways in which you, the teacher, can use skill sheets as you work toward improved instruction should be carefully studied. Skill sheets may be used for the sole purpose of noting the skills in which each child has achieved proficiency and/or they can be used to guide the teacher in a multi-text, language experience or individualized approach to learning. When the skill sheet is used in this manner, the teacher will be planning and teaching lessons with a variety of media which will always be emphasizing the basic skills of a subject area.

Skill sheets are being used in some schools as a means of more accurately reporting progress to parents. Frequently they are interpreted by the teacher at parent conferences and in some instances they are sent home either in place of the traditional report card or as a supplement to the report card.

It appears as though the utilization of skill sheets is broad, indeed, and creative teachers will discover more improved ways of using them to the advantage of our children.

Another evaluation form used extensively in today's nongraded school where individualization of instruction is stressed is the child's evaluation of independent study or research projects which he pursues on his own for depth study. The chart on page 172 illustrates the evaluation of a study on magnets. The evaluation form gives the child's name, experiment number, date started, date completed, and the number of the science packets, the topic studied, concepts learned, and the child's personal evaluation of the study along with the teacher's evaluation.

CONTINUOUS PROGRESS CHECK SHEET
FOR SOCIAL STUDIES UNIT

Progression unit Ages 7 and 8 Families and Their Needs	Understanding Social Skills and Study Skills	Evidence of Learning
Social Understandings and Attitudes		*Evaluation*
Understandings:	Families need shelter from rain or snow.	Diagnostic Tests
	They need shelter from cold or heat.	_____
	Families need to be safe and comfortable.	_____
	Families everywhere need food to eat.	_____
	Some families grow their own food.	Pupil, self-evaluation
	Some families buy food in stores.	_____
	Some families hunt and fish for food.	_____
	People need clothes.	_____
	People choose clothes that keep them comfortable.	_____
		Teacher evaluation of pupil
	Clothes worn outdoors might not be worn indoors.	_____
	Clothes worn in some lands might not be worn in others.	_____
	There are many families living on the earth.	_____

A LOOK AT REPORTING PRACTICES

CONTINUOUS PROGRESS CHECK SHEET FOR SOCIAL STUDIES UNIT
(con't.)

Progression unit Ages 7 and 8 Families and Their Needs	Understanding Social Skills and Study Skills	Evidence of Learning
Understandings: (continued)	People in families need rules.	1. Actions
	People in families need to plan.	_____
	The people in our nation help make the rules.	_____
	The leader of our nation is the President.	2. Attitudes
Social Skills:	Shares materials with other children.	
	Works well in large groups, small groups, and individually.	
	Contributes to group discussions.	
	Shares ideas and plans.	
Study Skills:	Knows where his home is on the community map.	
	Can find the United States on a world map.	
	Knows how to follow directions.	
	Can recall what he reads.	
	Can classify simple ideas.	

CHILD'S EVALUATION OF INDEPENDENT STUDY

<u>JIMMY JACKSON</u>
(name)

<u>Experiment 12</u>
(number)

I began <u>November 8</u> and completed <u>November 14</u> package <u>123</u>
      (date)   (date)   (number)

<u>MAGNETS</u>
(topic)

Major Concepts

Magnets attract metal.

Magnets have two poles, north and south.

The north pole attracts the south pole and the south pole attracts the north pole.

Magnets are useful in lifting loads.

A magnet is in a compass.

You can magnetize other metals.

Evaluation

Child's Evaluation

    I enjoyed making a compass with the cork and needle

Teacher's Evaluation

    Jimmy knows his work well—is ready for the next unit.

PUPIL PROGRESS REPORT

Even though parent-teacher conferences are held and cooperative studies of individualized skill sheets are made, many teachers and parents still prefer that a pupil progress report be sent home. Any school embarking on a nongraded program should develop a progress card which is consistent with its beliefs about children and how they learn and is representative of the philosophy of the nongraded school plan.

It is suggested that one individual conference period coincide with the issuance of the first report card. The purpose of the parent-teacher conference is to establish active two-way communication in reporting and appraising the child's progress and any factors affecting his progress. The following guidelines are offered as a possible means of translating pupil progress in the nongraded elementary school:

1. Scores on standardized language arts and mathematics tests, though imperfect, are helpful in diagnosing pupil achievement in conjunction with daily teacher assessment.

2. The grades sent home should be consistent with the philosophy of the school.

3. Grade cards used during the transitional period from a graded school to a nongraded school should indicate the number of years a pupil has been in school so that the grades assigned are fully intelligible in terms of the grade-level they represent.

4. Progress in the other areas of the curriculum should be reported to the parents in the same general manner as in language arts and mathematics—that is, in terms of the pupil's progress rather than as any percentage of a set course.

5. Report cards should identify and evaluate special talents in speaking, writing, music, art, leadership, and other areas.

6. Report cards should be diagnostic rather than judgmental in dealing with each child's progress and problems.

7. Some statements on the report card should seek to reinforce desirable behavior.

In brief, if report cards are to be used they should be consistent with the philosophy of the nongraded plan; they should reveal what we know about children and how they grow and develop. Reports should denote the level of progress which the child is achieving; and should tell how well he is achieving in the prescribed content and learning experiences designed personally for him.

The following illustrates types of report cards used in three nongraded school programs:

PARENT—TEACHER CONFERENCES

The parent-teacher conference is an important aspect of the reporting program. Conferences enable the parent and teacher to understand the child better. Parents should be informed concerning the purpose of the conference and what is expected of them. Adequate preparation for a conference should be made by the staff. Teachers should be informed on how to conduct the conference interview (for example, prepare for the conference by reviewing the cumulative record, make the parent feel welcome and comfortable, be alert to and aware of differences in cultural background, use tact as facts are presented, be professional at all times, keep confidences, place himself in the parent's position, avoid comparison of one child with another, avoid dealing in generalities, and listen closely and sympathetically).

Most nongraded schools are using conferences and/or report cards for informing parents of the child's progress. These conferences, skill sheets from different areas of the curriculum, examples of daily work, tapes from the child's daily language experiences, and other health, social, and emotional records of the child's life should be discussed. Follow-up letters, telephone calls, or home and school visits should accompany the conferences. On pages 175-188 are example forms used for conferences in nongraded schools.

Narrative Reporting

The use of narrative reporting is being employed in an increasing number of schools. The narrative report provides the teacher with an opportunity to write a statement concerning each child's progress in every curriculum area. A more individual and specific report results from this type of reporting. When narrative reporting is utilized, the following guidelines are suggested as a means of enabling teachers to report in a systematic way about all children to their parents. It is most desirable if a faculty plans these guidelines together for their particular situation.

PRIMARY REPORT CARD

MILWAUKEE PUBLIC SCHOOLS
PROGRESS REPORT
PRIMARY SCHOOL

To the Parents:

The educational welfare of children and youth is best served when there is complete understanding and cooperation between the home and the school. As a basis for such understanding and cooperation, the school prepares this report on your son's or daughter's progress. It will be sent to you three times each semester.

This report records student achievement. It also presents the best judgment of the school as to the growth that has taken place in those personal characteristics that make for good citizenship in the school and community.

It is hoped that parents will find time to study this report carefully. You are invited to confer with principals and teachers. The school will appreciate any comments from parents that will assist in meeting the needs of individual children.

Superintendent of Schools

Principal

Teacher

School

School Year 19__ 19__ Semester_____

Classification Next Semester _____

Side 1

PERSONAL AND SOCIAL GROWTH

Wherever you find a check ( ), your child needs to improve

	Report Period		
HEALTHFUL LIVING	1	2	3
Practices good health habits			
Observes safety rules			
PERSONAL DEVELOPMENT			
Plays well with others			
Respects rights of others			
Observes rules and regulations			
Shows growth in self-control			
Accepts responsibility			
WORK HABITS AND ATTITUDES			
Follows directions			
Completes work begun			
Works well independently			
Works well with others			

ATTENDANCE

	1	2	3		1	2	3
Days ABSENT				Times TARDY			

Side 2

A LOOK AT REPORTING PRACTICES 177

NAME

			SEMESTER ABOVE KINDERGARTEN				
1	2	3	4	5	6	7	8

GROWTH IN LEARNING AND SKILLS

Meaning of Marks:
    C--Is making good progress.
    D--Needs to improve.

This form or progress report covers a period of at least three years in the primary school. It takes time to recognize the learning power of each child. In these early years, growth may be rapid during one period and slow during another. Therefore, it seems wise to use a narrow marking system--2 symbols--until the growth and power can be more definitely determined. In the beginning each child will be marked in some areas but not in others.

                                              Report Period
READING   (see Progress Chart on Back of Card)   1   2   3
    Shows readiness for reading
    Reads with understanding
    Is acquiring needed reading skills
    Reads independently for pleasure
    Reads independently for information

LANGUAGE (Speaking, Writing, Listening)
    Shares ideas and experiences with others
    Expresses ideas clearly
    Responds well to stories and poetry
    Is a good listener
    Is acquiring skill in handwriting
    Is acquiring skill in spelling
    Writes his own stories and letters

ARITHMETIC
    Uses numbers with understanding
    Reasons well in solving problems
    Is acquiring number facts

Your child shows special interest in areas marked (X).

    Arts and Crafts   Science
    Music   Social Studies
    Stories and Poetry   Physical Education

Side 3

Reading Progress	
Level	Date
1	
2	
3	
4	
5	
6	
7	
8	
9	
10	
11	
12	

1. As children progress from Level to Level 12 the reading material becomes more difficult.

2. The latest date indicates the level on which the child is reading.

3. A conference between the parent and the teacher is desirable.

Remarks:

Date

I have studied this report.

1._____

2._____

3._____

Parent's Signature

Side 4

A LOOK AT REPORTING PRACTICES

NON-GRADED

PRIMARY PROGRESS REPORT

****

ABINGDON ELEMENTARY SCHOOL

Washington County
Abingdon, Virginia

19_____ 19_____

_____
PUPIL

_____
TEACHER

SUPERINTENDENT'S MESSAGE

 This is a report to you from the teacher concerning your child's progress in school and it deserves your careful examination. In case you find that your child is not making satisfactory progress, it is suggested that you discuss this very important matter with the teacher and offer suggestions for improvement. Best work can be done when teachers and parents work together in planning and directing the educational program of the child.
 Feel free to visit the school and offer your suggestions for the improvement of your child's progress in school.

      E. B. STANLEY, Superintendent
      Washington County Schools

	ATTENDANCE RECORD						
REPORT PERIOD	1	2	3	4	5	6	TOTALS
DAYS PRESENT							
DAYS ABSENT							
TIMES TARDY							

A LOOK AT REPORTING PRACTICES

STUDENT'S NAME

Key: V - Very Commendable
      G - Above Average
      S - Satisfactory
      I - Needs Improvement

SUBJECT	\multicolumn{4}{c	}{First Report}	\multicolumn{4}{c	}{Second Report}	\multicolumn{4}{c	}{Third Report}
	Level	Individual Achievement	Effort	Citizenship	Level	Individual Achievement	Effort	Citizenship	Level	Individual Achievement	Effort	Citizenship
HANDWRITING												
HEALTH & PHYS. ED.												
ARITHMETIC												
ENGLISH Oral Expression												
Written Expression												
Listening Skills												
SPELLING Assigned Words												
Written Work												
SCIENCE												
READING Oral												
Phonetic												
Comprehension												
ART												
MUSIC												
DESIRES CONFERENCE Teacher												
Parent												

A LOOK AT REPORTING PRACTICES

Level	Individual Achievement	Effort	Citizenship	Level	Individual Achievement	Effort	Citizenship	Level	Individual Achievement	Effort	Citizenship
Fourth	Report			Fifth	Report			Sixth	Report		

LEVEL: Where the child is working
Level 1 - Readiness
Level 2 - Pre-Primer
Level 3 - Primer
Level 4 - First
Level 5 - Second
Level 6 - Advanced Second
Level 7 - Third
Level 8 - Advanced Third

(E) ENRICHMENT: ADDITIONAL WORK

EFFORT: How much the child tries

INDIVIDUAL ACHIEVEMENT: What the child does in relation to his capability

CITIZENSHIP: Work habits and conduct
1. Needs to be more attentive
2. Needs to be more courteous
3. Needs to work more carefully
4. Needs to work more independently
5. Needs to obey school rules
6. Needs to respect rights and property of others
7. Needs to work and play well with others
8. Needs to assume responsibility
9. Needs to follow instruction
10. Needs to practice good health habits
11. Needs to practice good safety habits
12. Needs to complete oral and written assignments
13. Is making satisfactory progress in areas 1-12

Signature of Parent or Guardian

_____

_____

Signature of Parent or Guardian

_____

_____

Signature of Parent or Guardian

_____

_____

Signature of Parent or Guardian

_____

_____

Signature of Parent or Guardian

_____

_____

Assigned to Level_____ for 19_____ 19_____

Teacher's signature_____

A LOOK AT REPORTING PRACTICES

ST. CHARLES PUBLIC SCHOOLS

St. Charles, Missouri

BENTON CONTINUOUS PROGRESS SCHOOL

Year_____

Teacher_____

Principal_____

_____ Division

Year in school _____
(above kindergarten)

To the Parents or Guardians:

_____
Superintendent

A LOOK AT REPORTING PRACTICES

SOCIAL ATTITUDES AND WORK HABITS

	REPORTING PERIOD			
	1	2	3	4
Takes care of materials				
Follows directions				
Listens carefully				
Completes work on time				
Uses time wisely				
Works neatly				
Works independently				
Cooperates with other pupils				
Cooperates with teachers				
Is courteous to everybody				
Uses good table manners				
Behaves properly (a) in halls				
(b) in classroom (c) in cafeteria				
(d) on playground				
Is obedient				
Personal Hygiene				

(✓) = Needs improvement

Reading and Arithmetic Achievement
(at the time of reporting)

	Level	6	7	8	9	10	11	12	13	14
Reading	Basal	Book 2 Part 2	Bk. 3 Pt. 1	Bk. 3 Pt. 2	Bk. 4 Pt. 1	Bk. 4 Pt. 2	Bk. 5 Pt. 1	Bk. 5 Pt. 2	Bk. 6 Pt. 1	Bk. 6 Pt. 2
	Rep. Date									
Arithmetic	Basal	Book 2	Bk. 3	Bk. 3	Bk. 4	Bk. 4	Bk. 5	Bk. 5	Bk. 6	Bk. 6
	Rep.									

CHILD'S NAME _____

Scholastic Achievement

REPORTING PERIOD

	1				2				3				4			
	Very Good	Satisfactory	Weak	Unsatisfactory	Very Good	Satisfactory	Weak	Unsatisfactory	Very Good	Satisfactory	Weak	Unsatisfactory	Very Good	Satisfactory	Weak	Unsatisfactory
LANGUAGE ARTS																
Reading																
Comprehension																
Fluency in oral reading																
Speed in silent reading																
Word attack skills																
Handwriting																
Legibility																
Neatness																
Language																
Oral Expression																
Written Expression																
Listening																
Spelling																
Daily Assignments																
All Subjects																
MATHEMATICS																
Basic Skills																
Application																
SCIENCE																
HEALTH																
SOCIAL STUDIES																
PHYSICAL EDUCATION																
MUSIC																
Vocal																
Instrumental																
ART																

ATTENDANCE RECORD	1	2	3	4
Times Absent				
Times Tardy				

TEACHER'S COMMENTS:
1st Quarter

2nd Quarter

3rd Quarter

4th Quarter

PARENT'S COMMENTS:
1st Quarter

2nd Quarter

3rd Quarter

_____
Parent's signature

_____
Parent's signature

_____
Parents signature

CONFERENCE REPORTING

RECORD OF PARENT-TEACHER CONFERENCE

Name of child_____ Date_____

Persons present_____

CONFERENCE SUMMARY AND RECOMMENDATIONS:

Child needs

Child interests

Illustrative materials used

Teachers' plans

Parent plans

Parent attitudes

Areas discussed and most immediate needs determined:

Teacher's immediate plans or Parent's immediate plans or suggestions

Parent's attitudes (toward conference, child, school)

_____
Teacher's signature

_____
Parent's signature

CONFERENCE REQUEST FORM

Dear_____:

Is it convenient for you to come to the Crescent School for a conference _____ _____ _____ at _____
                     day   month   date   hour
o'clock?

We feel that the conference could be more beneficial if both parents are present. In some cases, we realize this is not possible.

Cordially yours,

------------------------------DETACH HERE----------------------------------

To the teacher:

I (will) (will not) be able to come for a conference on

_____ _____ _____ at _____ o'clock.
  day   month   date   hour

Cordially yours,

A LOOK AT REPORTING PRACTICES

FACULTY GUIDELINES FOR NARRATIVE REPORTING

1. Clearly state specific progress achieved in skills for reading, spelling, writing, English and mathematics.

2. Comment on any individual areas where the child experienced success. For example; (1) illustrated talk on summer trip to the Grand Canyon (2) spelling bee winner (3) independent research report on the history of the community (4) construction of a bulletin board display (5) creative booklet on "Signs of Winter" (6) serving as a good committee leader.

3. Indicate specific areas of weakness in particular skills.

4. If possible, provide suggestions for improving the skills through work that can be done at home with the parents.

5. Report units mastered in social studies and science and unique contributions the child made while studying these units.

6. Compile a brief statement concerning his strengths and areas where improvement is needed in behavior patterns. Perhaps a useful suggestion to parents for helping to teach the desired behavior. Behavior here is meant to include self-discipline, child's response to classroom teacher directed discipline, interaction with class members and appropriate general behavior for the child's age level.

7. Indicate special interests of the child in school.

8. Encourage a written reply from parents.

Reporting of this type obviously demands staggered reporting periods as it is impossible for teachers to write reports like this all at one time. The reporting period can be staggered over a one month period so that the teacher sends reports home for approximately seven children a week. The report is given to the child or mailed home on the day it is written by the teacher. Narrative reports are sent home twice a year and a parent-teacher conference is held for the last reporting period or whichever reporting period is most desirable for the personal contact. It should be noted here that some schools have started narrative reporting in one area of the curriculum only; thus moving into it more slowly and not consuming as much time as for all narrative reporting.

Limited experimentation has been carried out using tape recorders and dictaphones to which the teacher dictates a narrative report, and a secretary or an aide then types the report to be sent home.

This is a new concept in reporting which will be improved as teachers experiment with it. Obviously, narrative reporting is more time consuming than a typical report card, but it pays better dividends in terms of the detailed way you can report to parents about their individual child's progress in the mastery of school subjects.

TRANSFER RECORDS

A child leaving the nongraded school should have an appropriate concise record of his personal and academic growth sent to the new school. Cumulative records should accompany the short transfer record. Every school should develop a transfer record that is considered adequate by all teachers. Whatever the method of transmitting past and present information, the following should be included: (1) school achievement records, (2) level of achievement in all areas, (3) health records, (4) standardized test records, (5) suggested grade in which the child should be placed, (6) significant objective opinions by teachers, (7) personal history, and (8) any problems which have a definite bearing on school work. Each school will have additional information not mentioned here that it will want to include in a complete and comprehensive transfer record. The form on page 191 is a sample transfer record which would be enclosed with other significant information.

SUMMARY

In summary, records are essential for placing children in a continuous progress program as the child advances through the different learning experiences or areas of content. The types of records essential for placing the children in individualized learning experiences are those which provide an abundance of accurate and complete information that can be studied from the developmental point of view.

If report cards are used they should be consistent with the philosophy of continuous progress program; they should reveal what we know about children and how they grow and develop. These report cards should denote the behavior of the child as well as the

A LOOK AT REPORTING PRACTICES

TRANSFER RECORD

Name of Student_____ Sex_____

Date of Birth_____ parent or Guardian_____

of - _____(Address)_____

is transferred to_____

Original Entrance Date_____ Transfer Date_____

Total Days Present_____ Total Days Absent_____

_____Year in School   Present Reading Level & Series_____

Book_____Page_____

Present Mathematics Level_____ Book_____

Recommended Grade Placement_____

_____
Teacher

_____
Principal

level of progress the child is achieving in the prescribed content designed personally for him.

Parent teacher conferences are essential. Parents should be informed concerning the purpose of the conferences and a follow-up letter or telephone call should accompany the conference.

Narrative reports are being utilized too. These reports include information concerning progress achieved, suggestions for improving the skills, contributions the child made while studying, brief statements concerning his strengths, and areas where improvement in behavior is needed.

Children leaving a continuous progress school to a traditional classroom situation should have an appropriate concise record of his personal and academic growth sent to the new school. Cumulative records should accompany the short transfer record.

The importance of maintaining accurate up-to-date records in the nongraded school cannot be overemphasized. Since children will function at their own rate of growth in flexible grouping situations, a thorough system of reporting should compliment the plan. Adequate reporting records will help the children and their parents understand themselves better. They should have this understanding of themselves without regard to fixed standards.

8

The challenge of the nongraded school is as challenging as its technology. Machines can only help the children learn; people make the difference in what happens to them.

The Materials Center: Instructional Media for the Nongraded School

SERVICES PROVIDED BY THE MEDIA SPECIALISTS

Every nongraded school must develop a materials center if its instructional program is to be successful. Leadership is needed to coordinate its resources, point out its advantages, and get it into operation. The Instructional Materials Center (IMC) is a manifestation of the belief that individuals are taught. The instructional materials center is the place where a student can go to learn at his own rate and on his own level of understanding.

The instructional materials center is a place where ideas, in their multimedia and different forms are housed, used, and distributed to classrooms and laboratories throughout the nongraded school. The instructional materials center contains magazines, pamphlets, teaching units, books, films, filmstrips, maps, pictures, electronic tapes, recordings, slides, transparencies, mock-ups, programmed materials, dial access, computers, teaching machines, and other instructional media.

Schools must develop their own rate of priority for purchasing materials for the materials center when changing from graded to a continuous progress school. The rate of priority will depend upon the program, the size of the school, and the budget.

It is the nerve center of the nongraded schools' total instructional resources since the objective of the nongraded school is to individualize instruction. Essentially the center is a service agency for students and teachers to facilitate the teaching-learning process.

In accordance with the nongraded philosophy which dictates that learning is personalized, the center is the place where students can actively pursue meaningful and individual study projects. In the materials center students can be observed viewing films, listening at listening stations, working with computers or teaching machines, doing research papers, or observing plants and animals as they grow.

The materials center in the flexible school is a place of intellectual excitement; the role of the center in a multiphased curriculum should reflect the modern world. In other words, it is an environment where children are seeking answers to their everyday questions about the world and themselves.

Another function of the center is to serve as an agency to supplement and enrich the curriculum and to provide a materials center of learning for each child, faculty member, and auxiliary person in the school. The following practical suggestions need to be followed in planning a materials center for a multiphased educational program:

1. The media specialist must work with different instructional teams to compile lists of background readings and bibliographies to enrich units of work.

2. The media specialist must know the topic being pursued by each student. (*Examples:* transportation, atomic energy, astronomy, war, submarines, airplanes; the methods to be employed, special reports, projects).

3. The media specialist should clip articles pertaining to units being taught in the school and to build a vertical file of material not found in books and other media owned by the school.

4. The faculty and the media specialist must cooperate in the purchase of materials to insure that the reading level of each child in the school has been served. This means that the materials in the center will range from the kindergarten through the secondary school.

5. The media specialist directs lessons to acquaint the pupils with the use of the facilities of the (IMC). These lessons should be correlated with practical application in the classroom.

6. The media specialist must provide different types of printed and audio-visual media on different levels of achievement and interest.

7. The media specialist must organize the media so it can be accessible for use.

Selecting Material and Equipment

In the nongraded school, a number of people may select the materials—team teachers, subject matter consultants, department heads, or other supervisors, the director of curriculum, media specialists, and principals. Each will select the material relevant in a given area and compatible with the methodological teaching processes of the nongraded program.

The persons directly involved with the curriculum at the teacher-learner level should be the logical persons for selecting materials. At times the students should be involved in the selection process.

Evaluation of Media

Once the material is located for a given topic a preliminary evaluation is favorable, previews are arranged and it is given a careful check. The following factors should be considered:

1. Is it suitable for large groups, small groups, or individually?

2. Is the vocabulary and reading content adequate for the group that will use it?

3. Will it be used by a student, the teacher, or a specialist?

4. Is the media consistent with the philosophy of the nongraded school?

5. Will its use be consistent with the behavioral outcomes of the nongraded program?

6. Does it allow for student involvement?

7. Are the materials selected complementary or supplementary to the inquiry process?

Arrangement of Space

The recognition that diverse activities will go on in the flexible functioning (IMC) means that adequate space needs to be provided and arranged in functional ways for the center to be effective. Areas must be provided where students can work with teaching machines freely without interruption, and view films on filmstrips or listen to recordings and tapes at any time. Careful planning of individual and group work spaces in quiet and noise zones will make this possible (see Photo 8-1).

Electronic Carrels

The carrels should accommodate, or have built in, all new media of communication which a student may operate on his own or with another person. The carrels should have the following built-in media:

1. Filmstrip and slide projectors.

2. Small screen television.

3. Projection for 8mm cartridge films, both teacher made and commercially prepared.

4. Earphones for use with discs and tape recorders.

5. A dictionary and reference materials placed close-by the carrels.

Dry Carrels

General types of "dry" carrels should also be provided with simple enclosure to which the students bring various instructional material such as reference books, programmed material, teaching machines, independent study, and written reports. These carrels should be well-lighted and properly ventilated for comfort (see Photo 8-2).

THE MATERIALS CENTER 197

PHOTO 8-1 Bill Haddox Photography

PHOTO 8-2 Bill Haddox Photography

Types of Furniture

Tables for four to eight students are used less frequently than individual desks in instructional materials centers. The small desks can be arranged to make a larger work area when needed. Special equipment should be built into tables and carrels when possible. This requires less space and expense than special acoustical rooms and at the same time makes it possible for several children to listen to a single recording at the same time.

Location of the Materials Center

The (IMC) should be located so that easy access to its many resources is possible. Often the materials center is placed in the center of the building, in the middle of the schools' traffic. In most modern nongraded team teaching buildings all content areas or instructional divisions open to the materials center.

It is also sensible to have teachers' workrooms adjoin the (IMC) since this helps bring teaching teams as well as children and materials close together. Easy access to teachers will encourage students to seek conferences with their instructors. When students work in the same area with their teachers constructive supervision can be given students.

Modified Structures

A number of buildings designed for greater flexibility of school programs have utilized folding walls leading to the materials center. Some of these buildings are round, and walls between the segments of the "pie" can be opened or closed according to the learning activities designed for the children housed therein. There are also rectangular buildings with similar kinds of interiors, all having the materials center as the nerve center of the buildings.

Many newer schools are designed to include large instructional spaces with no walls opening or closing. Teachers and children work together in this large space as a team. Much of their material may be housed in this space, having a main materials center for resource media.

Organization of Materials

Effective coordination of material is characteristic of a good

THE MATERIALS CENTER

instructional materials center. The nerve center of the (IMC) is the central catalogue, the guide to every source of information and resource the nongraded school has as well as that of the community, e.g., resource persons, other city library materials, and some state and national resources.

Some materials centers use color coding on their reference cards. This method of coding lets students know through what media information is presented. For example, books may be on blue cards, transparencies on red cards, recordings on yellow cards; this allows the student to not only select the topic but he can also choose the media.

If media is placed in instructional areas e.g., science equipment, language arts materials, art media, music instruments, and mathematic devices, it should be included in the IMC catalogue so it can be used for special projects. The card catalogue gives their location in the building.

Two approaches are used for organizing materials in most materials centers. Some house all materials on one topic together, regardless of media; others organize items by the media. The method of organizing materials is not important. It is important that the catalogue is complete and understood by all who use it, and that the materials are easily available to students, teachers and auxiliary personnel.

Below are some goals for the media specialists to consider when organizing a materials center for a nongraded program. Listed also are some questions relating to each goal:

I. Materials Must Be Available:

   1. What kinds of media are necessary for a good teaching-learning situation in a nongraded program?

   2. What materials and resources are available in the community?

   3. What criteria should be used for selecting instructional media?

   4. Who should be involved in the selection of materials?

II. The Team Teachers, Specialists, and Auxiliary Personnel and Children Should Be Aware of the Different Kinds of Available Materials.

   1. How should the catalogue be organized to best serve the total school needs?

2. What is the function of the catalogue?

3. How can the total school be informed of the materials available within the school?

4. How can new teachers and aides be made aware of community resources?

5. What are the values of multi-media correlations?

III. Materials Must Be Provided for the Team Teachers, Auxiliary Personnel, and Children When Needed:

1. What are some effective ways of distributing materials from the materials center?

2. What procedures can be established which will aid the total school to order materials?

3. What equipment is essential for maintenance and storage of materials?

4. What record forms should be maintained in the Instructional Materials Center?

5. What services should be provided by the Center?

6. What are space requirements for an effective materials center?

IV. Team Teaching, Auxiliary Personnel, and Children Must be Aware of the Value of Various Kinds of Instructional Media and Know How to Use It Effectively:

1. How can the total school be assisted to acquire mechanical skills?

2. How can workshops be used to improve the use of media?

3. How can the total school be helped to evaluate their use of media?

4. What mechanical skills or competencies should the total school develop to use various kinds of materials and equipment?

5. What kind of in-service bulletin should be used? How should the bulletin be organized?

THE MATERIALS CENTER

V. Evaluation of the Media Center:

1. What types of instructional media should be used?

2. Are some phases of the evaluation best done by different school personnel?

3. What effect do in-service workshops have on the instructional program?

4. What criteria should be considered in evaluation of the program?

5. What is the relation of the "software" resources to the "hardware" resources? How are both used in the instructional program?

Information Retrieval System

In many IMC's the Information Retrieval System is an added feature. A camera is available to produce its own microfilm cards. Materials which are valuable enough to preserve are given the media specialist by the teachers so that they may be placed on microfilm. After they are microfilmed, the cards are coded and sent to the data processing office to be key-punched. When the cards are returned they are ready for viewing by the student on micro-card readers. A reader-primer is available for reprinting microfilm for use with small study groups or for individual study. The microfilm reader is used for reading back issues of magazines on microfilm.

Technical Processing Room

The learning resource center has a technical processing room. Equipment such as photo equipment, typewriters, duplicating equipment, tape recorders and other items of proven value should be located there.

In this portion of the learning resource center 8mm film loops, tapes, and photographs will be developed.

A copy machine should also be set up in the technical processing room for teachers and children to copy materials. Copies can be reproduced for children to use as reference for independent study and discussion. These machines are useful for duplicating magazine articles, mimeograph materials, and other printed matter.

EFFECTIVE PROGRAMMED MATERIAL FOR SKILL DEVELOPMENT

An increasing number of programmed materials is becoming commercially available in a variety of subject matter areas. Mere availability is no guarantee of equality, however.

Programs are being produced in a variety of forms. The majority of programs break the subject matter down into a large number of small steps or "frames" requiring the child to make one or more response to each step. Careful programming requires the programmer to take pains to insure that these steps embody a logical, well-sequenced progression of the subject matter.

Programmed materials are designed to adapt to individual differences by allowing each learner to proceed at his own rate.

Don Parker, in his book, *Schooling for Individual Excellence,* reported that in individualizing instruction in the basic skills through programmed material, two important things are accomplished: (1) the pupils learn better and faster than they do in group instruction: (2) the teacher's time is saved for the important work of being a learning consultant, and/or curriculum advisor.[1]

These programmed materials should be selected carefully by the media specialists and special area teachers before placing them in the materials center and/or classrooms to be used by the children.

INDIVIDUALIZED LEARNING KITS FOR INDEPENDENT STUDY

Individualized learning kits for science, language arts and social studies should be placed in the IMC for students to pursue independent projects on their own. Once the child has finished with the materials issued to him in the kit, he will return the kit to the check-out-desk where the next part of the assignment will be ready for him. It may be some sort of follow-up designed by the teacher or it may mean that the child has free time to choose something on his own because he has completed his work so rapidly.

These kits may contain worksheets, media for experimentation, books, charts, graphs, filmstrips, recordings, tapes, etc. What this does is to free the child to learn as a learner should, and it will free teachers to work effectively, that is, planning, diagnosing the

---

[1] Don Parker, *Schooling for Individual Excellence* (New York: Thomas Nelson and Sons, 1963), p. 181.

instructional problems and needs, and prescribing instructional applications.

These kits should contain materials suitable for use with the inquiry process. They will be used to help students find answers to their questions for which the students are seeking solutions. The materials in the kits are used for study purposes utilizing the single concept approach. They will also be suited to the user. The material in the kit must fit the student's comprehension level and suit the learning patterns of the individual.

COMPUTERS AND TEACHING MACHINES

Computers and teaching machines are used in some nongraded schools to help teachers individualize instruction. Recent research indicates that students at all age levels come to feel at home with this sort of equipment and are quite willing to make its use a part of their daily school experience.

Experiences with this type of technology cannot supplement the teacher's instruction, but these exercises can be presented to the student on an individualized basis. The brighter children could receive more difficult exercises; the slower learning children receiving easier ones. These tutorial systems allow teachers greater opportunity for personal interaction with students.

Teachers and administrators should be able to develop even closer relations in a setting where computers are used to aid instruction. The information gathering capacity of the computer enables administrators to have a much more detailed profile and "up-to-date" picture of the strengths and weaknesses of each area of the curriculum.

Computer-assisted instruction is possible with only one console in a materials center classroom which would be shared by many students during the day. In a more expensive and elaborate arrangement, a classroom or the materials center would have a large number of consoles, and each student could spend considerable time—as much as an hour and a half a day—at the console (see Photo 8-3).

The console will usually contain a typewriter keyboard that the student can use to "talk to" the computer and a television screen that can display written messages as well as simple drawings, graphic materials, and equations. The student has a "light pen" which he uses to select answers to the problems shown on the screen; he can even erase or change the images that appear. The computer talks to the student through a pair of earphones or a loud speaker which provides him with the verbal communication necessary for effective learning, particularly when new concepts are being presented.

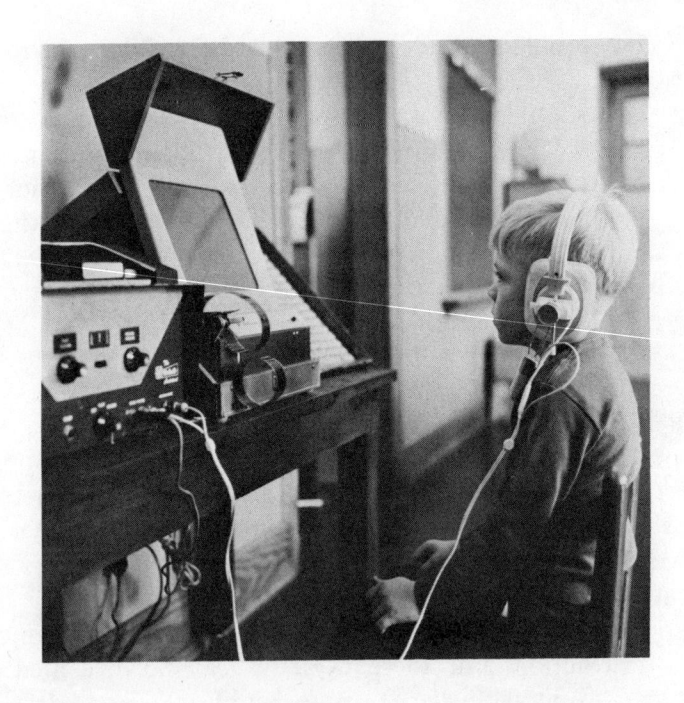

MULTI—PHASED TEXTS

It takes a very creative teacher to organize himself and his children to individualize instruction effectively in the nongraded school. The teacher needs to have *many more materials* than in any one basal program, that is if a basal program is used. A collection of varied textbooks and resource materials is essential. Not only are many varieties of texts necessary, but these textbooks should be selected on different reading abilities and levels.

The materials center should not only contain multi-phased texts but these materials should depict the different cultures of children portrayed in our society.

It is essential that more than ever before the materials center should contain current reading material to supplement the multi-phased texts which cannot depict current information. Such current reading materials as newspapers, magazines, comics, pamphlets,

THE MATERIALS CENTER

student current publications, and brochures should be included to use with basic textbooks.

T. V. TEACHING

Experiments have shown that students learn as much subject matter from instructional T.V. as they do in live or conventional classrooms. T.V. teaching along with other instructional media will be important factors in providing education of the scope and depth of the children in the nongraded elementary school. How else can the modern elementary school provide the necessary substance for the many kinds of interests, the increased enrollments, the rates of learning progress, the different learning styles, and the different goals of children?

For excellence in T.V. instruction, it takes the following competencies:

1. T.V. teaching should be done by the subject matter expert to give the students the best information possible.

2. There needs to be a producer who knows the extent of the effectiveness of the media, what to do to make the lessons interesting and challenging.

3. The media-specialists who have a great deal of skill in multi-media techniques should be included.

4. A teacher or cognitive psychologist who knows the needs and learning styles of the children who are to be involved in viewing the program should be a part of the team.

The T.V. sets can be placed in large group areas, in classrooms, or placed on portable carts to be used in the Materials Center or moved to other parts of the building.

T.V. scheduling is very essential in the nongraded school because of the flexibility of groups and individuals. It is imperative to coordinate programming of closed-circuit television in the nongraded school. There must be a close coordination of all production, channels, presentations, and television staff involved for the whole week. This recording of events is essential (see Photo 8-4).

Some schools are using small-designed, closed circuit T.V. portable

PHOTO 8-4

equipment designed for self-operating. It requires little or no equipment set-up time and allows the performer to do his own camera switching and to produce his own show without dependence upon anyone else.

VIEWING AND LISTENING MATERIALS

Viewing and listening materials offer many advantages for helping to individualize instruction. Films, filmstrips, slides, opaque projections, transparencies, speed machines, tapes, and recordings used alone as an audio-visual aid or as a multi-phased approach helps the child to not only personalize his instruction but enables him to better understand concepts presented.

Films and Filmstrips

These materials present a terrific challenge for the teacher attempting to individualize instruction. Films and filmstrips enable the teacher to bring the outside world into the classroom, and recreate in the classroom events that occurred anywhere in the world. Proper use calls for selection, utilization, and evaluation of films and filmstrips on the basis of information contained in the film or filmstrip, suitability to individual and group learning, and organization and quality.

Films and filmstrips are valuable for introducing new units, to raise problems for study or discussion, to develop interest and provide information. Films and filmstrips should be catalogued for distribution in the IMC. Lists of films and filmstrips from the central system and state should also be placed in the IMC Center for teachers to use.

Slides, Opaque Projections, and Transparencies

Still projections represent a large family of materials which have unique contributions to make in the teaching-learning process. These projections have so many practical applications they cannot be listed. They are especially useful for large group instruction presentations, for motivation and general information. They, too, are stored in the IMC for effective use by teaching teams.

Tachistoscope and Controlled Readers

These devices are used for individual instruction enabling children to increase speed in vocabulary and comprehension in skill subjects, especially reading. These machines can be stored in the IMC and checked out for use in the classrooms, in language arts laboratories, or could be placed in carrels for individualization of instruction in the Materials Center.

Pre-Recorded Lessons on Tape

The tapes serve to make more economical use of teachers' time as well as to individualize instruction for the children achieving at different levels. Some of the advantages of the use of tapes to help individualize instruction in the nongraded school are:

1. Tapes can be used for practice and drill.

2. Tapes yield to flexibility of grouping.

3. Pre-recorded tapes can be thought-provoking and challenging for the bright child.

4. Tapes help teachers individualize instruction on a large scale.

5. The teacher on the voice recorder brings the best diction to the student.

6. Tapes when used with the "read with me" method help slow students understand the content from books as the teacher explains the illustrations, new words, and concepts.

Each tape lesson contains the materials for a complete lesson to be used by one child, a small group of children, or by a large group of children. Prepackaged, pre-recorded lessons are developed by the school's instructional staff or purchased from commercial companies. Each lesson contains three basic features: (1) a guide for the teacher containing the content, the objectives of the lesson, instruction to the teacher and follow-up activities, (2) a reproduceable master of the student's response or worksheet which serves as a record of each child's understanding of the taped lesson, and (3) a tape recording which usually contains explicit oral directions that make full use of the student activity sheet or other available printed materials.

Some of the equipment currently used to implement the tape teaching program in the materials center or other instructional areas: (1) jackboxes, which contain multiple outlets for connecting earphones, (2) tape tables or carrels with jackboxes fastened to them, (3) tape recorders with proper size output jacks or external speaker jacks to match the jackbox plug and the earphone plug, and (4) earphones which enable the child to learn the program without disturbing other children involved in other classroom activities.

The instruction materials center operates a tape library on the same principle as a central film library. Team teachers as well as individual children make their selection from a catalogue and then request the tapes from the materials center.

Recordings

Learning experiences can be enhanced through the use of recordings by an individual at a listening station or can be a means of introducing a lesson in a large group situation. Recordings are also used with filmstrips and transparencies using a multi-media approach, thus offering both the audio and visual perception techniques for learning. The recordings should be recorded in the catalogue denoting if they are to be used with a filmstrip or other media.

VARIED REFERENCE TEXTS

Since most of the child's work in the nongraded school is pursued on his own rate and interest, varied reference texts will be essential to meet the various requests by individual students. Reference books should be placed close by the study carrels as the children seek answers to their problems. The reference texts should include those on modern technology, space, mathematics, science, literature, the arts, different atlases, dictionaries, world almanacs, and encyclopedias. These references, and more of the same types, are always available on the shelves. Reference materials should be revised yearly with up-to-date supplements (see Photo 8-5).

These materials find a promising place in the modern materials center because they (1) provide for individual differences in ability and interest, (2) help children develop problem-solving techniques, (3) enable students to answer questions that arise, and (4) present varied points of view on controversial issues.

As the materials center grows it can afford to secure additional useful references such as biographical dictionaries, dictionaries of familiar quotations, dictionaries of synonyms and antonyms, foreign languages, and dictionaries of scientific terms.

PHOTO 8-5   Bill Haddox Photography

MAPS, GLOBES AND MODELS; MODERN TRADE BOOKS

The children in the nongraded school working individually, in small groups, and in large group situations need various media to make concepts meaningful to them. Maps, globes, models, and modern trade books help children with numerous opportunities to read, observe, compare, gather data, analyze the data, and formulate concepts.

Maps

Large wall maps are essential for large group sessions; small maps are used for independent study and small group work. Maps should be selected for the materials center which depict particular features of an area to stress such as roads and economics. The map focuses on these features, leaving out other things such as political divisions or minerals. Hence different types of maps are needed to reach various educational goals in the nongraded school where goals are personalized to meet the needs of children.

Globes

Globes of all sizes, shapes, and description are effective learning tools in a nongraded program, especially where the curriculum is intended to expand beyond the classroom to include the world and into space. Globes of all types can be stored in the IMC for individuals and groups to use; they should also be placed in all content areas.

The kinds of globes most useful in classrooms are: (1) physical features of the earth's surface, (2) political boundaries, (3) both physical and political features, (4) mere outlines of major land areas on a slated surface which children and teachers may draw on, and (5) globes showing the surface of the moon.

A large globe suspended from above should be placed in large instructional areas, especially in the social studies areas. Smaller globes may be mounted on a plain table stand, in a cradle, or a stand with a meridian ring.

Models

Because a model gives a three-dimensional impression of some

THE MATERIALS CENTER

lifelike object, they are very helpful to children having trouble visualizing. Models help communicate to children the nature of things that are either too large, too far away, or too rare or complex to bring to the classroom.

Models also offer excellent media for making concepts meaningful whether they be used in a large group demonstration lesson or studied by an individual pursuing information on a independent project. The most common models used in the schools are those pertaining to the human body, insects, animals, the solar system, and rocks and minerals. A diorama is a special model that pictures a scene in three dimensions; a puppet is a model used in presenting a play.

These models can be catalogued in the materials center and checked out by the staff members or individuals as needed. If the models are kept in the IMC they can be accessible to more people.

Modern Trade Books

Modern trade books written on different levels of instruction are essential instructional tools for the nongraded school. The materials center in the nongraded school should contain many of these: novels, storybooks, biographies, travel books, adventure, and science. Such materials enable students (1) to find immediate answers to questions that arise in small group discussions, large group work, or in independent study, (2) to provide better for individual differences and interests, and (3) to be used in seminars for providing varied points of view on controversial issues. It is important to select some of the titles for reluctant readers containing a high interest level and low vocabulary. These books should have titles depicting functional, lifelike, experiences that are meaningful to this group of children (see Photo 8-6).

Trade books for the gifted child should also be in the materials center. These books should be catalogued and placed in the area for those children to use for small group discussions, scheduled seminars, and for individual reading. Some of these books are usually selected from the paperback editions and include many of the classics and novels which gifted children read so well.

In summary, the IMC covers a tremendous range in planning the communications facilities for flexible school programs. Components vary from simple projectors to T.V. cameras, reading-out displays, complex consoles, and varied printed programs.

Richard Phillips, Morgantown, West Virginia
PHOTO 8-6

Gone are the days when one ordered isolated pieces of equipment and plugged them into convenient outlets. Program planners are involved in a total systems approach to audio-visuals.

It is inevitable that at some point during the planning for a new flexible elementary school, educators should face up with some very basic questions, such as:

1. Are there to be study carrels? If so, what kind? Wet or Dry? Where will they be located?

2. How can provision be made to accommodate computerized instruction?

3. Should the large group instruction area have single or double screen projection?

4. Should T.V. be in a large group lecture area or in every classroom?

5. Is it practical to have subject-matter curriculum resource areas as well as a central materials center?

6. What about a dial access retrieval system? Where should it be located? Why?

7. What about microfilm teaching-learning?

The answer to such questions can no longer be left to afterthought until the materials center and new building is completed. As we plan new flexible nongraded programs for elementary schools we should include overall provisions that will permit virtually every space area to be gradually interconnected into an overall electric distribution system throughout the entire structure. These plans will eventually include a nationwide telecommunications network.

Thus, the enlarged instructional materials center or centers within the nongraded school of the seventies would permit sizeable numbers of children to work independently at wet and dry carrels with materials, both printed and technological, designed for them individually.

At the same time the media specialist and staff along with the teaching staff would be free to select the appropriate materials for use. They should also evaluate their impact upon individualization of instruction as well as learning in small and large group situations.

The IMC specialist and team leaders will always endeavor to use multi-media as an instructional technique. It is the author's desire that technology will not crowd-out the humanization of the curriculum, but enhance creativity and human relations. Instead of making education more technical, the mechanics should give educators a real opportunity to humanize teaching-learning situations.

9

Each human being is a combination of abilities and attitudes. This causes him to react in a variety of personal and impersonal ways.

Personalizing Instruction in the Nongraded School: Humanizing the Process

HOW TO MOTIVATE THE LEARNER

One of the problems in designing a curriculum for the nongraded school is finding the key which "turns on" students. The many successful attempts as illustrated by our drop-out problem in the nation denotes that the solution is not simple.

Individual motives range from extrinsic goals of wanting to be praised, accepted, and loved, to intrinsic needs for satisfaction of accomplishing a problem solving task. Bringing the right kind of task to the right kind of individual is the challenge for the nongraded school.

Schools have been fairly successful in relation to intrinsic motivation, especially that which deals with grade and reward achievement, and curiosity motivation. There is considerable interest now being focused on cognitive motivation stressing such concepts as creativity, inquiry, problem-solving, and discovery.

Following are some implications for motivating the student in the educational process:

1. Research reveals that when the child's desire to achieve is high, the mother used a strong positive reinforcement of warmth and approval for success, as well as a strong negative reinforcement for failure.

2. Difference in achievement among children in favor of middle and upper social class has also been established.

3. The middle and upper class parents expect high educational and occupational attainment, while lower class parents play down academic achievement and stress work.

4. Teacher and parent expectations may operate as a critical variable in affecting the performance of learners.

5. An increase of moral problems in the society may be characterized by high levels of achievement motivation.

6. A positive relationship between grades and high achievement with IQ have been fairly well established.

7. Lower class parents emphasize praise and tangible rewards as opposed to concepts and correctness.

8. Learning may be accelerated when the probability of failure and grades are removed from the learning environment.

The following recommendations are suggested as concrete ways in which the nongraded school might motivate children:

1. Elementary guidance programs should be offered in the school for counseling children needing help.

2. A careful diagnostic system designed to determine individual needs and a prescribed curriculum to complement these needs is essential.

3. Provision in the curriculum development where group-oriented cooperation is considered which includes all types of children is imperative.

4. Lifting the fear of failure in the classroom is essential for increasing motivation.

5. Modification of the curriculum and methods to suit the learning style of each individual is imperative.

6. Encouragement of the child's achievement through parent counseling and educational instruction is recommended.

PRESCRIBING THE SKILLS NEEDED

We live in an age of analysis. Educators along with others are attempting to synthesize and systematize everything. We analyze in order to understand, solve, or improve the problem. These processes are some of the essentials of our changing to chronological society. Therefore, nongraded school, caught in this change, must make an analysis before prescribing the skills needed for each child if individualized instruction is to be achieved.

Recognizing and meeting the intellectual as well as the emotional and social needs of children for today and tomorrow's world, leading toward developing the creative potential, have become imperative purposes of education in the modern elementary school.

Since many factors enter into this process of analysis as indicated in Chapter Two of this book, prescribing the skills needed for the individual child is not an easy task, that is if the creative potential is to be developed along with the intellectual skills.

The modern school will give more attention to the model of the cognitive domain which stresses the sequential classification from low to high order thinking processes. Educators who have stressed the cognitive domain advocate that later operations are built upon earlier ones, and that intellectual development follows an ordered sequence. They say that a child is incapable of learning these higher level thought processes before earlier ones are mastered, e.g., synthesizing, inventing, transforming, relating, designing, and hypothesizing.

Therefore, we must be certain that skills prescribed have a close parallel between the development of the intellectual functions and the emotional and social development of the child since both must be in accord for effective living.

Educators prescribing the skill to be learned must include attitudes, values, appreciations, and feelings since most educators believe that thinking processes cannot operate effectively without these.

It must be understood that the better a child feels about the content, the more interested he becomes, at his developmental level, to want to learn more about it. This also holds true, the more he knows about something, the more he appreciates it. Therefore, when prescribing skills to be learned, there must be a combination of both cognitive and emotional feelings involved for effective human development.

It is imperative to plan learning experiences in the modern nongraded school where the pupils' behavior become goals or objectives within themselves. These experiences must cause the child to think, feel, and enjoy every experience in the curriculum. In other words, the content cannot be separated from how the child thinks about it.

Since changing behavior is the primary target of every teacher, then the first thing we must do is analyze the behavior the child possesses when he comes to us as well as that behavior we wish him to exhibit after he has been taught. In order to modify behavior in a systematic way we need a series of behavioral objectives which are appropriate for the child to perform.

Adequate observational records must be kept of the child's responses and the methods being used. This also gives the teacher feedback with respect to changes in teaching. If there are too many errors, the teacher must restructure the instructional activity so that there will be an increase in the child's performance.

FREEING THE LEARNER TO LEARN ON HIS OWN

It is quite likely that the self-starting ability of the child or the desire to "learn on his own" is hindered by overly detailed supervision by parents and teachers. It is also hoped that *too much* reliance will not be placed on prescribed curricula in the nongraded team teaching school. The emphasis should be placed on the effort to appraise and credit growth resulting from the student's own initiative.

Perhaps we would develop a higher level of creative thinking if we did not try to teach too many subjects and allowed times for self-initiated learning, thinking creatively about the subject taught, and the like.

Children will enjoy working on their own if they are rewarded for this type of work. If teachers, counselors, and parents base their evaluation on the memorization of details, students will memorize the texts and lectures. If grades are based upon ability to integrate and apply principles, they will attempt to do this. If you give credit for the development of original ideas and for self-initiated learning, they will develop original ideas and engage in self-initiated learning.

It is obviously important that children have available the resources for working out some of their ideas when working alone. Otherwise, frustration and a feeling of purposelessness are likely to result. There is value in the experience of seeing one's values in some concrete form or product. It is also important that teachers and parents utilize the resources of the community in stimulating children to work on their own.

To obtain the greatest results "learning to learn on your own" must be supplemented by the development of skills in research on how to learn, e.g., how to use the card catalogue, finding and evaluating information, recording and classifying facts, outlining the content, and determining the style of writing. This means that the child should begin to develop research skills early in his school experience and should require them both in depth and breadth. The development of these skills should be accepted consciously as an instructional goal in the nongraded school.

The children should also be encouraged to utilize the public library, museums, factories, farms, recreational facilities, service institutions, and the like for seeking answers to their questions.

It is equally obvious that the instructional media in nongraded school resource centers and even the community will not provide all the resources which children will need to carry out their ideas. They should be taught the unavailability of resources, and learn to improvise. It should be pointed out that there is an important difference between accepting limitations and accepting them creatively. It should also be stressed to the child working on his own that there may be several solutions to a problem, and that many are still unsolved. Children should recognize problems of the physical world as external so that they do not appear as personal obligations or as failures if they are not solved.

DEVELOPING A SELF CONCEPT

The nongraded school stresses the worth of the individual and encourages all children to value themselves as individuals.

Research has shown that self is one's reflected appraisal that others think of him, and the major factor in understanding the behavior of another person is to understand how that person perceives himself. Therefore, educators must understand that a child cannot behave independently of the way he thinks about himself.

The nongraded school should create an atmosphere which accepts the child as he is. According to some psychologists, as one moves toward a more positive view of self he becomes more open to his experience and is more capable of understanding himself.

If the child can present the person he really is to the group, he is under much less strain, because he has only one self to keep up with. If on the other hand, he has to fabricate a self to present to the group he must be careful at all times that he is presenting that self to the group rather than the self he feels he really is. This keeps him on guard, saps his strength, causes him to withdraw, and inhibits any spontaneity of behavior.

Therefore, team teachers in the nongraded school must coordinate the learning activities of all children and diagnose the children frequently for behavioral patterns. For what a child thinks of himself, both consciously and unconsciously, is the prime determiner of his behavior. A child who thinks of himself as competent, courageous, friendly, is characterized by behavior in accord with these conceptions. On the other hand, a person who views himself as inferior, reserved, cowardly, unlovable, cannot help behaving in such a way.

The modern nongraded school has a responsibility to help develop a desirable self-concept. Since the first years of life are the most important for developing the self-image with each successive year becoming less important, it must start there. The self-image is seen to be structured by adolescence, and after this, one's self becomes less subject to modification by the "significant others" around him. Next to the family, the responsibility for developing a good self-image of the child lays upon the elementary school.

In the quest for self, therefore, the team should utilize the resources of all the staff members, perceiving themselves as positive persons and be able to form affectionate relationships with those they teach. They have a job to accomplish among themselves, therefore, before they can begin to work on others. It is time teachers begin valuing themselves at their real worth, for no one will begin to esteem teachers at their true value until teachers value themselves and their work highly. The organization of the nongraded team teaching school encourages the rewarding of both the child's and teacher's self-image.

Teachers must be aware that the child brings his self-concept to class with him. He teaches the child who he is, what he is while teaching subject matter. In helping to build a good self-concept the teacher should not teach the child what he should be, but try to help him become what he may be.

The following is a brief list of educational practices which should be of value in strengthening one's concept of self-worth in the nongraded school:

1. Each child should be given tasks to do which are appropriate to his level of competence.

2. Emphasis on the individual should be more important than emphasis on knowledge.

3. An atmosphere of warmth, acceptance, and respect should be present among the team members.

4. Assessment should be on an individual basis.

5. Positive encouragement should replace negative remarks.

6. Children should be placed with different types of children in the learning environment in order not to be branded as "slow," "bright," "disadvantaged," or "middle class."

KEEPING THE CREATIVE SPARK ALIVE

One of the most widely accepted objectives of the modern school is to teach the child to test reality; to give them a realistic picture of the world in which they live.

In training children to test their ideas and those of others against reality will also serve to safeguard us against some of the creativity which should be legitimately looked upon with suspicion. This should safeguard us against brainwashing, fascism, rioting, hate, and the like.

Research, especially that performed by Torrance has emphasized some important ways the school might be sensitive to the creative child. It is imperative that the school recognize the following when attempting to understand the creative individual: (1) his problem of coping with the sanctions of society against divergency; (2) being alienated of one's friends through the expression of a talent; (3) pressures to be well-rounded; (4) fear of being criticized as being different from sex-rate norms: (5) having a desire to want to learn on one's own; (6) attempting tasks which are too difficult; (7) searching for a purpose in life; (8) having different values and being motivated by different rewards; and (9) searching for one's uniquenesses.[1] Running throughout all of these problems, of course, are factors which lead to psychological withdrawal from society, parents, teachers, and the peer group.

Schools have not always rewarded the creative student because he has not always "fitted into the mold." The following assumptions underlying creativity follow and need to be recognized by educators:

1. Creativity is not limited to the so-called "gifted."

2. Creativity is shown in many diverse fields and aspects of life, and in different ways.

3. Creativity is not limited to the arts or any special field.

4. There are environmental conditions which favor creative potential.

5. In the face of a rapidly changing society, creative ways for change are needed.

6. Creativity can be fostered and developed in all children within limits.

Developing a Creative Classroom Atmosphere

In the creative classroom there is an atmosphere of "released control," permissiveness, a sense of security, an absence of fear, flexible working conditions, and the like.

The classroom group may also stimulate certain types of creative thinking. Children should learn early that creative ideas are shared

---

[1] E. Paul Torrance. Problems in Maintaining Creativity. *Guiding Creative Talent*. Prentice-Hall, Inc., Englewood Cliffs, New Jersey. 1963. pp. 108-121.

and enjoyed by the group; they very effectively learn on the ideas of one another.

Teachers and auxiliary personnel have many opportunities to create situations which require children to do creative thinking. At all levels of the nongraded school, the necessity for creative thinking can be created by making the problems given students sufficiently difficult in relation to the subject. This challenge kept on a high level of difficulty cannot be maintained continously, but occasionally every individual should confront problems which stretch his imagination and ingenuity to the limits.

All teachers in the nongraded school should attempt to apply the following principles for creating an environment for creative experiences. Torrance[2] urges all teachers to seek systematically and consciously to apply them in a reasonable and appropriate way:

1. Treat questions with respect; try to help the child find his answers to questions.

2. Treat imaginative ideas with respect; do not make fun of the child's ideas or conclusions from his experiences.

3. Show your pupils that their ideas have value. Have them write down their ideas; adapt some of them or try them out in classroom activities; display them on the bulletin board.

4. Occasionally have pupils do something "for practice" without the threat of evaluation, to try something out, and later to do a similar task for the record for keeps.

5. Tie in evaluation with cause and consequences. In criticizing defects in ideas or in punishing naughty or dangerous behavior, explain the response in such a way as to foster the ability to see causes and consequences of behavior.

All of these principles must, of course, be applied within the limitations of the age group one teaches. The applications should be continued and consistent rather than just "one-shot" treatments.

The teacher who respects ideas is usually different from the person who prides himself in a highly planned organized classroom organization. The willingness to be flexible in scheduling in the

---

[2] *Ibid.*, pp. 142-161.

nongraded school is essential for the development of an environment which develops the creative spark in children. Levels, phases, and flexible schedules can also become barriers to the creative process; they may even encourage rigidity.

Provide Time to be Creative

The history of invention and discovery show that quiet periods of relaxation are also conducive to creative thinking. A child is not likely to be able to give way to his wishes, dreams, or fantasy, and produce creative ideas in a busy, structured, teacher-dominated classroom. Children should have an opportunity in the nongraded flexible school to do something alone and not have to participate in a group every minute of the day. Allow them to read to themselves, do creative writing, draw and paint, experiment and invent, and even rest at times; the quiet way may be an aid to creative thinking.

It is suggested that the modern flexible school for mental health reasons at least provide space in every classroom for children to work alone when the need arises. Such a proposal could be supported as a possible condition for developing creative thinking. Many of the modern schools are building "little theaters" for children to participate in dramatic plays.

Humanizing the Curriculum

In the nongraded school with its flexibility and respect for the individual, there are ample provisions for building humanization right into the curriculum; wholesome human feelings are integrated into every phase of the child's learning experience.

A great portion of the child's daily experience should be open-ended, explanation and discovery, with nothing guaranteed, instead of giving or asking the child to find pat answers. In a creative environment, and with the right kind of staff, we might produce a different kind of person. It is the way the curriculum is used that does it.

A curriculum is not something a child learns; it is the instrument you teach with. What happens to the learner while he is learning, his discovery, his feelings, his attitudes, and his social skills, are always more important than the content. These are the things that "live on" after content is forgotten.

In the nongraded school, the staff should study the conditions which facilitate learning; they must realize that the most important of these conditions is the attitude between the facilitator and learner.

Following are other conditions which are imperative if the learner is comfortable within his learning environment:

1. The learner must be free to find his own answers.

2. The facilitator must be willing to live the thoughts being expressed.

3. There must be a respect and trust for the learner.

4. There needs to be a classroom situation in which the differences of children are honored.

5. The environment for at least a portion of the day, if not all day, should be free, self-initiated, and spontaneous.

6. The student-student relationship should be more aware, more sensitive, and more concerned about others as well as a self-seeking learning situation.

7. There must be a concern for matters of meaning, sensitivity, and how things look to the child, whatever is pursued in the classroom.

8. There should be more commitment and involvement in the planning and implementation of every aspect of the educational experience of the child.

9. Team members should be awarded for humanizing the curriculum or for rewarding personal meaning.

10. Humanization of education is a concern of all staff members in the nongraded school, e.g., administrators, teachers, specialists, and auxiliary personnel.

In attempting to humanize the environment for children, the school must represent the model for allowing students to experiment with being themselves. This will take a courageous, trusting, and compassionate staff.

Although the modern nongraded school will become increasingly automated, this technology should not make the classroom less humanized. Teachers should let these machines teach the routine skills; allow the automation to release human energy. But do not expect it to make life challenging, interesting, self-fulfilling, and rich in varied experiences. This calls for creative teaching! The extent of our peace, security, and interpersonal existence, is the process of education. Teachers are not computers stored with knowledge to "give out" when a child needs it; they are seeking, planning, and encouraging children, finding challenges, and new values where old ones seem "worn out" or have lost their usefulness.

ENCOURAGING INQUIRY AND EXPERIMENTATION

A program of mass education has resulted in structured rigidity and in placing a premium upon conformity. Nevertheless, there is much to indicate that in the nongraded school with skillful teaching and corresponding educational objectives, mass education need not destroy either the joy of inquiry or the thrill of experimentation.

The nongraded school is organized on the assumption that inquiry and experimentation should be encouraged. In the nongraded situation, one explores the premise that all minds, irrespective of their ability, are active rather than inert and can create and invent as well as react. The nongraded school seeks to develop confidence and imagination in its students so that learning takes on new meaning through inquiry and experimentation.

Inquiry and experimentation involves the process of forming ideas or hypotheses, testing hypotheses, and communicating the results to others. Implied in this definition is the creation of something new, something which one has never seen or something which has never existed. This involves creative and adventurous thinking; breaking out of the mold. It leads one into the unknown. Included in this process are such things as discovery, imagination, explanation, invention, observing, experimenting, and curiosity.

Today's child goes forth into a much larger and uncertain world. Inquiry and experimentation is a way the child satisfies his curiosities. He is essentially raising questions and seeking answers, and he must if he is to survive.

Unfortunately, the traditional school or the modern world makes little provision for being understood by children.

Teachers in the modern school with flexible furniture, mass media, and more freedom are in a unique position to use the child's questions as the organizing center for activities which help him learn the beginning of inquiry skills. Such efforts will be effective to the degree that the teacher gives careful consideration to all elements involved in instruction: objectives, methods and procedures, materials, and evaluation.

Several conditions must be met if the child is to raise questions:

1. There must be a classroom climate that is open to his queries.

2. The child must be made to feel comfortable concerning his questions.

3. He must have assurance that other children will listen to his questions.

4. The child must know that some of his questions will be considered for action.

5. The child should be encouraged and rewarded for asking questions.

The teachers in the nongraded school must stimulate curiosities in areas which are not commonly available to the child, e.g., those occurring outside of the school; those involving the unknown presented through pictures, drama, music, print, and audio-visuals.

Problems pertaining to all kinds of subject matter and all types of human activity should be included in the child's learning experience. Problems that are somewhat fixed and static in nature as well as changeable; problems that are real and stem from personal humanity are to be solved also by the children. This will require of the individual a fairly high level of critical and logical thinking. Can the school of tomorrow expect less?

Teaching through inquiry and experimentation is a very valid means for teaching the objectives of critical thinking, problem-solving, and decision making. It is also an excellent way to provide variety in the classroom schedule. If used effectively, it can and does produce excellent results.

WORKING TOGETHER IN MULTI—CULTURAL GROUPS

Man's social and cultural evaluation is proceeding at an extraordinary pace. Mass media and recent publications help to make clear the way in which this new revolution is affecting us. We are still trying to understand each other in spite of the divisions. It is only through understanding of each other that the world, fit for life, can be developed. The modern elementary school must endeavor to meet this challenge.

In the nongraded school, the following recommendations are suggested for grouping children from all cultural backgrounds. It is also suggested that the main objectives for grouping and regrouping children in the nongraded school are to (1) build the self concept, (2) free the child to be an individual, (3) to prepare the child to live effectively in a changing society, and (4) to help build the communication skills.

The recommendations follow:

1. Human relations will develop most effectively when there are a great variety of ways which children of different ethnic groups engage in common activities on a one-to-one basis. Such attitudes and relations are basic to the development of our society.

2. Since all children must learn under the most positive set of human interactions, teachers should be teamed for instructional groups, being warm and supportive to all children.

3. A major effort must be made to identify the children having a difficult time with their instructional program and offer tutorial help as needed, increased counseling, and help in the basic skills.

4. Materials should be adopted to the children's state of readiness and provide the skills and experiences they lack.

5. Schools involved in teaching multi-cultural groups should prevail upon lay personnel to interpret the efforts of the schools to the community and to obtain community reactions.

6. Stable grouping situations should be organized for the children having trouble adjusting to flexible schedules, that is until they have adjusted to flexibility of movement.

7. Small classes for skill development, stressing the perceptional skills should be organized for children having language development problems.

8. Provision should be made for children from different cultural groups to meet in seminars to discuss current issues, e.g., civil rights, peace, justice, brotherhood, law enforcement, Americanism, Communism, rebellion, and community planning.

9. Every effort should be made to study the children from different ethnic backgrounds in order to determine if the scores from IQ tests give an estimate of mental ability which is often an injustice to these students as far as actual ability is concerned, and that perceptional training remedies some of the handicaps which influence performance of many children from different ethnic groups on IQ tests.

10. The nongraded program should be certain that the school's extra-curricular program be organized to fit the children from different socio-economic and ethnic backgrounds.

11. Auxiliary personnel should be selected from different ethnic groups so the children can identify with some adult from their environment.

12. Material should be selected which depicts the multi-ethnic children; their place in the present society as well as what they have contributed to the world.

13. Special guidance services should be provided and combined with intensive instruction so that students can recognize the need for wanting to succeed for children needing this extra help.

14. Pre-school programs should be organized to promote cognitive abilities, impart basic information and modify attitudes which are essential for academic success.

Programs must be developed which will deal realistically with the problem of the actual needs of multi-cultural groups while not freezing lines in American society. Schools must combine a high degree of individualization with consequent adaptations of the curriculum, with every effort being made that each child regardless of color, race, religion, or socio-economic backgrounds might develop to his fullest potential.

SUMMARY

In summary, there are concerns such as the following for the schools of the future: (1) a real interest focused on cognitive motivation stressing such concepts as creativity, inquiry, problem solving, and discovery; (2) emphasis is being placed on the effort to appraise and credit growth resulting from the child's own achievement; (3) the school has a responsibility for developing a good self-image of the child, therefore, team teachers must coordinate the learning activities of all children and diagnose the children frequently for behavioral patterns; (4) the school must be sensitive to the creative child; (5) human relations and the humanization of the school must have top priority and there will have to be more concern with people than only with subject matter; and (6) programs must be developed that deal realistically with the problem of the actual needs of multicultural groups.

10

The dogmas of the quiet past are inadequate ... disenthral yourself ... cut loose from old traditions and begin to make new ones.

Abraham Lincoln

Program Evaluation and Communication

ABSOLUTE ESSENTIALS

Since nongraded programs are an integral part of the total educational program it is necessary to evaluate the purposes of the program to assure that they are in harmony with the general purposes of education. In evaluating the nongraded program, consideration should be given to personnel, curriculum, grouping structures, grouping children, and program development. Inherent in all these elements and of primary concern, however, is evaluation of the progress of the individual toward the achievement of both general and specific educational goals. Such progress can be judged if the purposes are stated in terms of the behavior expected of each individual, if situations are identified and created in which individuals can work toward achieving this expected behavior, and if appropriate procedures are used to collect data on pupil progress.

PROGRAM EVALUATION AND COMMUNICATION

The type of educational program demanded now requires a better understanding of the nature of the learning process, a close identification of education with the demands of living in a democratic society, and the development of teaching procedures taking into account the broad objectives of the modern elementary school.

The term evaluation should refer to the accumulation and interpretation of comprehensive evidence concerning the abilities, status and problems of children by means of formal as well as informal procedures. It includes also the accumulation and interpretation of evidence concerning teaching techniques and methods, curriculum and school facilities. Instructional practice growing out of a newer psychology of learning should emphasize the modification of behavior, continuous growth, multiple learning and insight. In keeping with this concept of learning, evaluation is concerned not only with subject matter learned or not learned but with attitudes, interest, work habits, physical development and personal-social development as well.

The general purposes of evaluation are as follows:

1. To reveal to teachers what is happening to each child educationally and psychologically;

2. To motivate learning by furnishing students information concerning success in various areas of the curriculum;

3. To furnish teachers with a means of appraising teaching methods, textbooks and other instruments of the educative process;

4. To provide a basis for continuous improvement of the curriculum and organization of the school;

5. To determine the progress the school program is making toward the achievement of accepted objectives;

6. To give students, parents and lay people an opportunity to evaluate the program.

The following are suggested questions that were developed from the general purposes of evaluation to use as criteria for evaluating a new program.

1. Educational and psychological progress of child

    A. Has the child progressed satisfactorily according to his level of ability?

    B. Are curriculum provisions adequate for the slow, average, gifted, and remedial students?

    C. Does the program challenge all students?

    D. Is adequate provision made for individual as well as group instruction?

    E. Are children emotionally well adjusted to school?

    F. Are children adjusted socially?

    G. Are children's interests being met at their level?

    H. Are some students frustrated by some aspects of the program?

    I. Do students accept the program?

2. Providing students with information concerning their success

    A. Do children see check sheets?

    B. Are check sheets adequate?

    C. Is grading system adequate?

    D. Is grade card adequate?

    E. Is grade card easily understood?

    F. Are students given the opportunity for self-evaluation?

3. Appraising teaching methods, textbooks, materials and effectiveness of personnel

    A. Are teaching methods meeting objectives?

    B. Is the school staff adequate?

PROGRAM EVALUATION AND COMMUNICATION

   C. Are special teachers used efficiently and effectively?

   D. Are physical facilities adequate?

   E. Are textbooks adequate?

   F. Are supplies adequate?

   G. Is teacher orientation adequate?

   H. Is in-service training of teachers adequate?

   I. Are standardized tests used?

   J. Are standarized tests adequate?

   K. Is the evaluation of program continuous?

4. Improvement of curriculum and organization

   A. Does curriculum meet the needs of all the children?

   B. Does the music, art, physical education, etc., curriculum meet the objectives of the program?

   C. Is teacher-student ratio compatible with good instruction?

   D. Are methods of grouping adequate?

   E. Does grouping provide for the continuous growth of individual students?

   F. Are provisions made for regrouping?

   G. Do students move from room to room with a minimum of confusion?

   H. Are there articulation problems for new students?

   I. Are there articulation problems for students leaving the school district?

   J. Are there articulation problems at the Junior High?

5. Achievement of stated objectives

   A. Does the program provide an opportunity for each child to begin at his own level?

   B. Does the program provide an opportunity for each child to progress at the rate suited to his needs?

   C. Does program provide instruction for each child in all areas of the curriculum?

   D. Does grouping provide for continuous growth of all students?

   E. Does program develop the potential of each student?

   F. Does program stimulate creative inquiry?

   G. Does program cultivate the higher mental processes?

   H. Does program encourage decision making?

   I. Does program develop skill in problem solving?

6. Evaluation of the program by students, parents and lay people

   A. Are students, parents and lay people encouraged to evaluate the program?

   B. Do students, parents and lay people feel free to evaluate the program?

   C. Is an instrument available for students, parents and lay people to use as a guide for evaluation?

   D. Are public and parents kept informed about the program?

TECHNIQUES USED FOR ASSESSING PROGRAMS

Effective evaluation can take place when purposes are defined in terms of specific program elements and individual behavioral outcomes. Some changes in behavior should be evident if an instructional program has been successful.

Grouping situations should be created in which the desired behavior can take place. In evaluating the behavior of children, a variety of situations should be observed. Since changes in behavior should be stressed, some effective means of collecting data on the specific quantity and quality of the change should be used. Evaluation in the nongraded elementary school will be enhanced by (1) recording anecdotal information regarding children's behavior, (2) observing children as they play and work with other children in the classroom, (3) observing children as they participate in social affairs, (4) observing physical activities of children at play and at work, and (5) securing records of daily academic performance.

In evaluating the nongraded plan of organization, behavior can be measured up to a certain point by means of standardized instruments. These instruments will yield information regarding achievement, readiness, and intelligence levels of children in the nongraded program. Each school must develop their own design for most effective use of this information. It is imperative that the aforementioned techniques for securing evaluative data are not used in isolation, but rather that they are used in combination to present a total picture. Each technique yields some specific amount of information and when compiled will present an accurate, comprehensive assessment of the new school plan.

FACTORS TO BE INCLUDED IN THE EVALUATION

A major factor in nongraded evaluation is the development of a questionnaire to guide the faculty in their assessment of the new program. The questionnaire should be designed in the planning stage of the new plan and then improved as the program is implemented. A thoughtful examination of the questionnaire on pages 236-238 will illustrate the importance of a device such as this in guiding the overall evaluation of the nongraded program.

Any deep study of the questionnaire on pages 236-238 will reveal both its practicality and its incompleteness for a specific school. As suggested, the means, the form, the check-list, or other instruments used for evaluation must be developed from the objectives, aims, and purposes of the program. It may, or perhaps should, reflect the central aspects of skill development, content, expected behaviors, attitudes, pupil industry, etc. But in no case will it be either accurate

FACULTY QUESTIONNAIRE
ON THE CONTINUOUS PROGRESS PLAN

	no	to a small extent	to some extent	to a large extent
Have the stated objectives and aims been reached?				
Is the school's concern for the structure based on an acceptance of a philosophy of education which recognizes individual differences?				
Are there clearly stated objectives, aims, and policies for the program?				
Is the program planned in such a way that it provides continuity throughout the child's school program?				
Is the program system-wide encompassing all areas of the curriculum?				
Is the program planned so that research techniques can be used to determine the weakness and strength of the program?				

NOTE: Just to check a list like the above means nothing apart from supporting data. For example, adequate appraisal in terms of "stated objectives" requires a deliberate accounting of specific actions, events, habits, etc. that may be used to support the selected answer.

PROGRAM EVALUATION AND COMMUNICATION

	no	to a small extent	to some extent	to a large extent

On Identification and Placement . . . . .

Do the grouping structures actually meet the need of the students?

Does the program include a systematic and comprehensive program for identification and grouping?

Is the grouping organization concerned with a variety of interests, abilities, and achievement levels?

Does the program make provision for the remedial student, underachiever, talented, and slow learner?

On Organizational Variations and Curriculum Provisions . . . . . .

Does the structure provide for skill getting development in language arts, and mathematics?

Is the child's work suited to the level of his ability?

Are there specific curriculum provisions made for all children — the slow, gifted, remedial, etc.

Does the program attempt to challenge all children so that they may develop to their potential?

Is there a distinct and separate time set up during the school day for problem solving, critical thinking, and creative experiences?

	no	to a small extent	to some extent	to a large extent
To what extent is there a systematic method for individualized, large group, and small group instruction?				

On Pupil Progress and Reporting....

	no	to a small extent	to some extent	to a large extent
Can the pupil actually see his own level of progress on the skill sheets provided for his continuous progress in the skill development areas?				
Are provisions made for the continuous evaluation of the curriculum in terms of the pupil growth?				
Are the students given the opportunity to evaluate their own program?				
Is achievement recorded at the level of the abilities of the children participating in the program rather than at the average, norm or standard for the groups?				
Does the program provide for a grading system which is consistent with the organizational and grouping structures?				

On Interpretation....

	no	to a small extent	to some extent	to a large extent
Are teachers, lay people, and students kept fully informed about the program?				
Is there evidence of teacher, parent, administrator, and student co-operation in the program?				

or valuable unless it is a deliberate reflection of what the program is intended to do.

ASSESSING ADMINISTRATIVE CHANGE IN SCHOOL INNOVATION

It is most beneficial to assess the types of change which takes place in the administrative structure of a school when new programs and organizational patterns are implemented. A rating scale can be designed to assess administrative change in a continuous progress plan, and it will provide administrators with valuable insights regarding teacher perception of their roles. The sample scale presented here can be effectively used by teachers attempting new programs.

ADMINISTRATIVE CHANGE RATING SCALE

Questionnaire for teachers working with principals who are/were involved in studying, planning, developing, or implementing new educational programs during the current/past year.

To Teachers: Think of the behavior of your principal last year and this year regarding the following activities; please compare his behavior and indicate your opinion by using the following scale:

1 — Indicates you have no basis for making a comparison or judgment.

2 — Indicates your principal does this behavior more frequently this year than last year.

3 — Indicates your principal performs about the same.

4 — Indicates your principal does this function less often this year than last year.

This year my principal: *Rating*

A. Is willing to permit teachers to determine the way teacher aides may be utilized. _____

B. Is willing to allow teachers more freedom during lunch. _____

C. Requires students to be very quiet in hallways and lunchroom. _____

D. Involves teachers in curriculum decision-making. _____

E. Is willing to allow flexibility in grouping of children. _____

F. Involves teachers in selecting materials. _____

G. Requires furniture to be in the same place each day. _____

H. Gives teachers planning time during the day. _____

I. Encourages more individualized instruction. _____

J. Requires teachers to be more diagnostic. _____

K. Informs parents on curriculum innovations. _____

L. Requires some change in reporting practices. _____

M. Involves teachers in in-service programs. _____

N. Requires parent conferences. _____

O. Is willing to change the program when the teachers feel that it is not working. _____

P. Is open to suggestion by others on ways to improve instruction. _____

VISITOR OPINIONAIRE

Another means of securing evaluative information concerning your new school program is the utilization of a visitor opinionaire. An evaluation of this type provides a school staff with valuable observer reactions to new practices.

The following opinionaire model provides an example of the types of information which might be yielded.

1. School visited _____

2. Date of observation _____

3. Visitor's title (mother, teacher, etc.) _____

4. Length of total observation _____

Please use the following scale to rate each activity or place which you observed during your visit.

5. *Excellent*—the provisions or materials are extensive and are functioning excellently.

4. *Very Good*—
   a. the provisions or materials are extensive and are functioning well.
   b. the provisions or materials are moderately extensive, but are functioning excellently.

3. *Good*—the provisions or materials are moderately extensive and are functioning well.

2. *Fair*—
   a. the provisions or materials are moderately extensive, but are functioning poorly.
   b. the provisions or materials are limited in extent, but are functioning well.

1. *Poor*—the provisions or materials are limited in extent and are functioning poorly.

M. *Missing*—the provisions or materials are missing, but needed; if present, they would make a contribution to the educational needs of the youth involved.

* If visitors wish to be more specific on No.'s 2 and 4, they may indicate the appropriate condition—a or b.

_____ Arithmetic	_____ Reading
_____ Art	_____ Science
_____ Language Arts	_____ Social Studies
_____ Resource Center	_____ Physical Education

Please check either *yes* or *no* for each question.

yes ____ no ____ 1. Is the instructional materials center or library well-equipped with such supplementary materials as tapes, slides, records, teaching machines, films, etc.?

yes ____ no ____ 2. Are these materials readily accessible to both students and teachers?

yes ____ no ____ 3. Do the materials adequately supplement each subject?

yes ____ no ____ 4. Do the materials on each subject come on varying levels of difficulty?

yes ____ no ____ 5. Does the materials center include self-teaching devices?

yes ____ no ____ 6. Are the materials in this center used frequently by the students?

yes ____ no ____ 7. Do students make use of materials other than texts?

yes ____ no ____ 8. Did you notice many students working independently?

yes ____ no ____ 9. Did you see a great deal of instruction which involved the entire class?

yes ____ no ____ 10. Did the students work cooperatively together in small groups?

yes ____ no ____ 11. Did the teachers seem to encourage questions, pursuit of individual interests and problems?

yes ____ no ____ 12. Was the structure of the classrooms flexible?

yes ____ no ____ 13. Did the teachers try to relate all areas of study?

yes ____ no ____ 14. Was there evidence that the teachers were continuously diagnosing the students?

yes ____ no ____ 15. Did the teachers seem to know exactly what each child needed?

yes ____ no ____ 16. Did the teachers seem to be aware of the social, emotional, and physical needs of the children?

yes ____ no ____ 17. Were the children appropriately grouped with other children of approximately the same achievement level?

yes ____ no ____ 18. Did the children appear relaxed?

yes ____ no ____ 19. Did the varying age levels of the students within one classroom appear to disrupt the learning process in any way?

yes ____ no ____ 20. Was there a wide variety of activities open to the students?

yes ____ no ____ 21. Were the children given the decision of selecting and planning some class activities?

yes ____ no ____ 22. Did the wide variety of activities occurring simultaneously within some rooms prevent effective working on the part of the students?

yes ____ no ____ 23. Did the teachers treat the children as individuals?

yes ____ no ____ 24. Did the children seem to enjoy what they were doing?

yes ____ no ____ 25. Were the problems which were presented to the students realistic and meaningful?

yes ____ no ____ 26. Did the children appear to be less dependent upon their textbooks?

yes ____ no ____ 27. Do you think that by letting each student work at his own speed, we have encouraged laziness?

yes ____ no ____ 28. Do you think that the children have above-normal intellectual curiosity (for their age) because of our non-graded program?

yes ____ no ____ 29. Does some degree of success appear to be within the reach of all students?

yes ____ no ____ 30. Do you think that our non-graded program will produce more adaptable individuals?

ADDITIONAL COMMENTS:

PERSONS INVOLVED IN THE PROCESS

As discussed throughout this book, each child is evaluated continuously on a one-to-one basis in the nongraded school. Careful evaluation is essential for each child if continuous progress is to be assured, to accomplish this objective, coordinated efforts of all persons involved in the program are essential.

Parents, teachers and children as well should understand the evaluative process, and all should enter into it to some extent. Elementary guidance counselors, specialists and curriculum directors should be directly involved at different levels of the evaluation process. In addition, research personnel should administer tests and interpret the results. Both subjective and objective judgment should be assessed by appropriate specialists.

Every person who participates in the formal evaluation should process the following competencies: (1) knowledge of research design, (2) general knowledge of educational objectives, (3) understanding of the function of the nongraded school, (4) knowledge of content being taught, (5) knowledge of measuring instruments, and (6) an understanding of methods of devising instruments.

In summary, if nongraded programs are to be an integral part of the total educational system, it is important to evaluate the purposes of the program, personnel, curriculum, grouping structures, criteria for grouping, program development, and dissemination of information concerning the program. It is also essential that these efforts be evaluated effectively.

INNOVATIVE PROGRAMS DEMAND EXCELLENT PUBLIC RELATIONS

Involve college education departments, local school boards, administrators, teachers, parents, and children.

Educational experiences will be extended and enriched through cooperative school and community relationships. The enthusiastic help of the community combined with the academic strengths of the complete school system could offer each child a better chance to learn regardless of school location, pupil population, socio-economic background, or cultural heritage of the children involved in the program.

Many people can contribute to the correct interpretation of new school programs. College education departments, school boards, administrators, teachers, and parents must actively participate to inform the public about innovative programs. There are a multitude of ways in which this can be accomplished.

Prior to the initiation of the nongraded program in any school, it is of utmost importance that the community (especially parents) have the opportunity to become oriented to the philosophy and operation of such a program. The degree of success of this plan is directly related to community orientation toward the program. Some parents should, therefore, be involved in the study of the nongraded program at the same time the faculty is in the study phase. Various orientation procedures should be utilized as the program is being planned and initiated:

1. Hold meetings for the parents who will have children involved in the program, especially during the spring prior to the beginning of the school year in which the program is to be initiated.

2. Have present at these meetings members of the central administrative staff, the principal, and a committee of teachers who will be working on the program to discuss with the parents such matters as (a) the philosophy of the nongraded program, (b) reasons for adopting it, (c) similarities and differences between graded and nongraded programs, (d) how the children will be grouped, (e) how progress will be reported, and (f) types of materials to be used.

3. Hold supplementary meetings during the year for the following purposes: (a) to discuss progress of the program, (b) to evaluate the progress, (c) to discuss parents' questions, and (d) to project future plans.

4. Send home at least one newsletter each semester to inform the parents of such matters as: (a) new development of the program, (b) impending changes, and (c) evaluative procedures.

5. Encourage parents to react to the program and to give their suggestions through conferences or written statements.

6. Develop a handbook for parents explaining the nongraded program by covering such matters as: (a) purposes of the program, (b) organization of the program, (c) advantages of the program for parents, teachers, and children, (d) methods for reporting progress to parents, and (e) list of materials for parents to read and use individually and in study groups.

Following is a speech given by the principal of Benton Elementary School to parents and interested members of the community before initiating the program.

PRINCIPAL'S SPEECH FOR BENTON SCHOOL PARENTS AND OTHER INTERESTED MEMBERS OF THE COMMUNITY
ST. CHARLES, MISSOURI

The Benton Teachers of the St. Charles Public Schools spent six weeks during the summer of 1966 in intensive study and planning a nongraded school for the children.

The Philosophy of the Benton Faculty is to accept each child on his immediate level of achievement and progress with him in a Continuous Progress Program.

The Philosophy is based on the following beliefs:

1. Each child differs in growth patterns.

2. Each child develops at his own rate, physically, mentally and socially.

3. A stimulating environment be provided so that each child will experience success at the various levels where he is working.

4. Every child should be guided to meet failures that will eventually come to him sometime during his lifetime.

5. Experiences should be provided that will instill in each child a desire for learning which comes from real and definite needs.

6. Opportunities shall be provided to prepare each child to live in a democracy where self-direction and problem solving are necessary.

7. A child learns better in a relaxed atmosphere without undue stress and strain.

We have chosen the name "Continuous Progress School" as we want success for each child, eliminating yearly repetition and failure. We want

PROGRAM EVALUATION AND COMMUNICATION

each child to develop his potentialities to the fullest extent. It is our desire to provide meaningful experiences for all children. We want each child to become a self-directing individual. To make this possible, we expect to carry out the following objectives:

1. To provide for the physical, mental, emotional, and social differences of children.

2. To provide opportunities for children to progress at their own rate of learning.

3. To group children so that they have opportunities to experience success.

4. To challenge each child to achieve according to his abilities.

5. To provide flexibility in a program for the changing needs of each individual.

6. To free pupils and teachers from undue and continuous pressures and maintain a favorable climate for learning.

7. To concentrate teacher planning for better instructional responsibility in each phase of the curriculum.

In our Continuous Progress plan we have divided our school into three divisions:

1. The Skills Division for children in their first and second year of school.

2. The Transition Division for children in their third and fourth year of school.

3. Refinement Division for children in their fifth and sixth year of school.

Each child will be permitted to progress at his own rate and will not be pushed beyond his ability to achieve. The Continuous Progress Plan is based on the child's achievement.

In a given division, each child has specific skills to master. As he progresses he is moved to the next division when he is ready. This is determined by conferences with the parent, teacher and principal.

In the graded school each child is expected to master the same skills in the same length of time. Each child is passed or failed at the end of the year.

In our Continuous Progress Plan children are grouped in a division or section of the division where they can make the most progress.

The children were grouped according to Achievement Scores and teacher judgment, based on social, mental and physical readiness for learning.

A child entering "The Continuous Progress School" will be placed in a group where it is believed he will succeed, but he will be changed to another group if it is found first placement did not meet his needs.

If a child leaves the "Continuous Progress School" and enters a Graded School, his achievement will be translated into graded terms and he will be placed in a given grade according to the achievement he has made.

When you visit a classroom you will see that the method of teaching has not changed, but more attention is given to the individual child. Good teaching, regardless of the program, is the key to a successful learning situation.

Most children will advance from the Skills Division to the Transition Division in two years (kindergarten not included in this), while some may require three years.

There may be a few children who will complete the elementary school in five years—others will take six years (the normal progress), or still others may take seven years.

As stated before, good public relations is essential in initiating a nongraded program. Following is an article published in the *Banner News*, St. Charles, Missouri, concerning the initiation of a nongraded program in St. Charles. The following type of information is distributed to parents to acquaint them with nongraded programs.

(PLAN STUDY ON EDUCATION PROGRESS PROGRAM HERE)

Area Teachers Will Participate in Workshop to Consider Feasibility of Continuous Progress Program for Elementary School Students

A group of 28 teachers from the parochial and public elementary schools of St. Charles are taking part in a six week workshop this summer.

The purpose of the workshop is to study the feasibility of the implementation of a continuous progress education program at the elementary school level. The workshop is made possible through the Federal Government under Title III of the Elementary and Secondary Education Act.

Mrs. Jane Wilhour, Director of the Child Development Laboratory at Lindenwood College, is serving as director of the St. Charles nongraded workshop. Consultants from various parts of the U.S. are being brought to St. Charles to present their views and experiences relating to the continuous progress program. These consultants are college professors, school administrators and teachers who have a knowledgeable background and experience with this type of educational program.

The basic philosophy of the continuous progress program is derived from the fact that all children do not progress educationally at the same rate. Some make rapid progress while others make slower progress than the average student.

In the past, a given group of students in the classroom were presented a fixed or prescribed amount of instruction usually geared to the median level of the group, the result being that the more capable students were not challenged and the less capable students became frustrated.

In the continuous progress plan each student is taught at the level and rate at which he can achieve the maximum amount of educational growth according to his capabilities. In this way each student can develop his capabilities to the fullest. It is hoped that this will eliminate the frustration experienced by the less capable student and also provide a means of challenging the most capable student, while at the same time the average student's educational needs will continue to be met.

Actually the continuous progress philosophy is not new. Various innovations of the program, of which the ungraded primary is one, have been in progress for many years in various parts of the country. Arrangements are being made for various members of the workshop to visit schools that now have in operation the continuous progress educational program. Some of the better known and successful continuous progress schools in the U.S. are in Florida, California, Tennessee and Wisconsin.

Throughout each school year it is vital to consistently plan for community orientation. It must be noted that communication programs are to be presented for parents as well as all other community members. Each day we should be more cognizant of the need to inform all community members of the school system's progress as it is the entire community that we ask to support our schools through their taxes.

Administrators, board members, faculty members and parents can cooperatively present local radio and television programs which will acquaint the public with school innovations.

Opportunities can be provided for teachers and administrators to speak at community service club meetings in order to secure their support for school innovations. Speeches of this nature will be more informative if they are accompanied by slides showing children in the school and/or by tapes of children's responses to questions about their new school programs. Responses to questions of this type are often revealing and enjoyable. The authors are reminded of the many times they have asked children why they like to change groups and move from one classroom to another, and with children's characteristic candor come the most frequently heard responses "We like to have more than one teacher and it's fun to get up and walk around."

Children can make posters for store windows in a city's business district that will show what they like best about their school. A child's drawing attracts many people and it will also give them a message about a school, thus directing the attention of the public to their school.

All teachers and parents are very much aware of the ways in which children act as mini public relations agents in regard to the schools. It is important for us to investigate new ways in which they might communicate the school program to the public.

The idea of an "Innovations Teach In," is another successful approach to informing the public of school programs. A "teach in" must be tailored to the needs and resources of each individual community, but it does provide an excellent opportunity in school public relations. A thorough review of the program developed by the authors for a "teach in" will stimulate your own ideas as well as showing you, the reader, the comprehensiveness of the day's activities.

INDIVIDUAL INSTRUCTION TEACH IN

Saturday, January 15   9:00 – 12:00

9:00 a.m. – 9:30 a.m.   "Our School"–Slide Presentation by Instructional Materials Center Coordinator

9:30 a.m. – 10:00 a.m.   "Individualized Instruction–What It Means to Your Child" by Professor, Department of Education

10:00 a.m. – 10:30 a.m.   Coffee and Doughnuts
                          Informal Opportunity to Talk with Faculty, Administration, and Board

10:30 a.m. – 11:00 a.m.   "Classroom Demonstrations of Individualized Teaching and Learning" by Teachers and Pupils

11:00 a.m. – 11:30 a.m. Tour of School Building by the Principal. An opportunity to view learning environments and projects of individual children.

11:30 a.m. – 12:00 p.m. "What Individualized Instruction Means for Our Children"–Panel Discussion by Selected Parents

12:00 p.m. – 1:00 p.m. Lunch in School Cafeteria and Opportunity to Talk with Teachers

A "teach in" provides a concentrated time in which all members of the community can learn together. It also develops pride in the city's young people and their schools. Your faculties will reap benefits far beyond their expectations when this type of public relations is utilized.

After considering a variety of ways to engage all community members in public relations it is necessary to heed one word of caution. Some innovative schools become too concerned with orienting the public and consequently they have no time to engage in continuous program improvement. This is a most unfortunate situation and encourages deserved criticism. In other words, no school should be so busy entertaining observers that they do not have time to evaluate and improve their program.

SUMMARY

In summary, this chapter reflected the evaluation of the objectives of the continuous progress program. It also depicted, in the portion of the chapter concerning evaluation of individualized programs for children, a concern for them as human beings.

The Continuous Progress school, when properly evaluated, will make a favorable impact on the child if the community is to seek the best possible education for its children in a changing society. The school and community must communicate the changes in behavior of the children as well as that of program development if the principle of equal opportunity for all children is to be retained.

These activities must be continuously evaluated and communicated to the public.

All human resources are needed to help children learn in realistic settings appropriate to their interests and needs, e.g., university education departments, boards of education, administrators, teachers, parents, and the community.

It is imperative for educators and citizens of the community to invent creative, flexible programs built around the needs of the children as well as those of society. Individualization of instruction with a thrust toward humanization is essential for excellence in education. The bridge between intention and accomplishment must be narrowed. This is the challenge for better schools in the future.

Index

A

A Handbook For Teachers, 26n
Abingdon Elementary School, 64, 155
  in-service education program, example of, 33-35
"Academic Package," use of in McNeill Elementary School, 27-28
Acceleration, 63-64
Achievement grouping, 61-63
Administrative change in school innovation, assessing, 239-244
Aims, hoped-for, of flexible school organization, 22-23
Anderson, Robert H., 107, 108n, 142, 142n
Appalachian Advance, 74-75, 75n
Application blank for teacher aide, model of, 151-152
Arithmetic skill sheet, model of, 165-166
Artificial subject matter lines, elimination of in nongraded program, 130-131
Arts, teaching of in nongraded program, 125-126
Arts specialists, role of in nongraded program, 139
Auxiliary personnel, need for and selection of, 140-150

Auxiliary Personnel, need for and selection of (*Cont.*)
  application blank, model of, 151-152
  benefits of, 148
  clerical aide, 143
  "do's and don'ts," 144
  factors causing need, 142-143
  materials aide, 143
  and public relations, 144-145
  selection of, 148-150
    ethics of profession, 150
    requirements, basic, 149
    talents and skills, special, 149
    volunteer aide, 150
  tasks for, 146-148
  teacher aide, 143
  teacher-teacher aide relations, 145-146
"Average" child, not "individual" child as focus of graded system, 22

B

Barger Elementary School, 83
"Behavioral Independence Level," meaning of, 27n
Benson, Charles S., 142, 142n
Benton Elementary School, 61-63, 65-67, 246
Byrd, Bob, 96

INDEX

C

Canady, Dr. Lyn, 74-75, 75n, 87
Carrels, electronic, 196
  dry, 196
Catalogue, central, as "nerve center" of nongraded school, 199
Cate, Mrs. Amendia Carroll, 87
Changing from graded structure to flexible nongraded program, 17-36
  change as inevitable, 17
  "average" child, not "individual" child, as focus of graded system, 22
  conclusions formed from experience, 21
  examples of effective nongraded schools, five, 25-30
    Fairview Elementary School, 25-26
    Harris School, 30
    McAnnulty Elementary School, 26-27
    McNeill Elementary School, 27-28
    Tusculum View Elementary School, 28-30
  flexible organizations, need for, 22-23
    aims, hoped for, 22-23
  framework for change, 23-25
  graded school, fallacy of, 19-21
    reasons for organization of, 19-20
  planning, 31-35
    Abingdon, Virginia, in-service education program, 33-35
    cooperation, broad base of, 31-32
    knowledge of nongraded programs, 32-33
    responsibility, fixing, 32
  summary, 35-36
Check sheets, information from to diagnose child's needs, 39-41

Check sheets, personalized, 161-172
  child's evaluation of independent study, model of, 172
  for mathematics, model of, 165-166
  for reading, model of, 164
  for science, model of, 167-168
  for social studies, model of, 170-171
Child's evaluation of independent study, model of, 172
Classroom atmosphere, developing creative, 221-223
  humanizing curriculum, 223-225
  time for creativity, providing, 223
Clerical aides, 143
Cognitive motivation, 214
Color coding in materials centers, 199
Community relationships essential for success of new program, 244-251
Community resources, encouraging child to use for independent study, 218
  utilizing in nongraded program, 158-159
  considerations, basic, 159
Computers in materials center, 203-204
Concept of self, developing, 218-220
  practices, recommended, 220
Conferences between parent and teacher, 174-190
Controlled readers, 207
Cooperation, broad base of needed in planning change, 31-32
Cooperative planning by staff of nongraded program, 134-136
  problems, solving, 135
Coordination as key function of principal in developing nongraded program, 136
Creative spark in children, keeping alive, 220-225
  classroom atmosphere, 221-223
  time for creativity, providing, 223

INDEX

Creative spark in children, keeping alive (*Cont.*)
  humanizing curriculum, 223-225
  problems, 221
Crescent Elementary Nongraded School, 140
Criteria, general, for grouping, 56-59
  list of, suggested, 58
Criterion and standard, difference between, 56
Cumulative record, 161
Curriculum in nongraded school, 106-133
  how to teach content, 127-129
  integration of subject matter into broad learning units, 130-131
  occupational world, training in skills necessary for, 128-129
  organizing for instruction, 131-132
  professional objectives, 106-108
  scope and sequence, including, 129-130
  summary, 133
  teacher, role of, 132-133
    personalized process, learning as, 132
    as resource person, 132-133
  what to teach, 108-111
    arts, 125-126
    health and physical education, 123-125
    language arts, 108-109
    mathematics, 109-110
    music, 126
    science, 110-111
    social studies, 121-123

D

Dangers in diagnosing children's needs, 52-53
Descriptive Bulletin on Operational Design of the Individualized Learning Center, 28n

Diagnosing children's needs prior to instruction grouping, 37-54
  check sheets, 39-41
  Diagnostic Information Sheet, model of, 38
  disadvantaged children, 51
  gifted, 50-51
  individualization, planning for, 46-47
    weekly assignments, 47, 49-50
  observations, 39
  pitfalls, 52-53
  self-evaluation, 41-44
  summary, 53-54
  tests, 44-46
  underachievers, 51-52
Dilenowisco Educational Cooperative Center, 155
Diorama, meaning of, 211
Disadvantaged children, 51
"Do's and don'ts" for teacher aides, 144
Dry carrels, 196
Dyersburg Elementary School, 67

E

East Stone Gap Elementary School, 94
East Tennessee State University, 29
Educational Professional Development Act, 155
Electronic carrels, 196
Elementary School Reorganization: The Current Scene, 18n
Equipment, selection of, 195
Ethics of profession, acquainting aide with, 150
Evaluation of media, 195-196
Evaluation of program, and communication, 230-252
  administrative change, 239-244
  essentials, 230-234
  purposes of, 231

Evaluation of program and communication (*Cont.*)
essentials (*Cont.*)
  questions as criteria for evaluation, 232-234
  factors, 235-239
  faculty questionnaire, 235-238
  persons involved, 244
  public relations, need for, 244-251
  "Teach In" as method of informing community, 250-251
  summary, 251-252
  techniques used, 234-235
Examples of effective nongraded schools, five, 25-30
Experimentation by children, encouraging, 225-226

F

Faculty questionnaire for evaluation of new program, 235-238
Fairview Elementary School as example of effective nongraded school, 25-26, 94
Fantini, Mario D., 18, 18*n*
Field trips into community, planning into nongraded program, 158-159
  considerations, basic, 159
Films and filmstrips, 206-207
Flexibility as keynote of grouping, 61, 132
Flexible organizations, need for, 22-23
  aims, hoped for, 22-23
Foreign language specialists, role of in nongraded program, 140
Framework for change in school organization, 23-25
Furniture, types of for materials center, 198

G

Gifted children, 50-51
Gilberts, Robert, 140
Globes in materials center, 210
Goodlad, John I., 107, 108*n*
Graded school, fallacy of, 19-21
  reasons for organization of, 19-20
Grouping as basis for nongraded school organization, 55-72
  criteria, general, 56-59
    list of, suggested, 58
  flexibility as keynote, 61
  function, how to make, 59-67
    acceleration, 63-64
    achievement grouping, 61-63
    heterogeneous grouping, 64-67
    pupil placement information, 59, 60
  and regrouping in flexible schedule, 71
  summary, 71-72
  team teaching approach, nongraded, 67-70
    individualization of instruction, 67-68
    organizational plan in continuous progress school, model of, 70
    schedule, model of, 69
Guidance counselor, role of in nongraded program, 139
Guidelines for functioning of team teaching, 84-87
Guiding Creative Talent, 220*n*, 222*n*

H

Harris School as example of nongraded organization, 30, 39-41
Health, teaching of in nongraded situation, 123-125
Heterogeneous grouping, 64-67
Hillson, Maurice, 18, 18*n*

INDEX

How to teach content in nongraded program, 127-129
Humanizing curriculum, 223-225
Humanizing process of instruction in nongraded school, 214-229
(see also "Personalizing instruction in nongraded school")

I

"In-basket" technique for learning technique in in-service program, 154
Independent study and team teaching, 82-84
Independent study, model of child's evaluation of, 172
Individualization, planning for, 46-47
  weekly assignments, 47, 49-50
Individually Prescribed Instruction, meaning of, 26-27, 68
Inevitability of change in school system, 17
Information Retrieval Center in materials center, 201
Initiative in learning, 217-218
"Innovations Teach In" as method of informing public about innovations, 250-251
Inquiry and experimentation, encouraging in nongraded school, 225-226
In-service program for total staff, 150-158
  experiences to be included, 153
  objectives, 153-154
  techniques for learning, 154-158
    in-basket, 154
    inter-group reaction, 155-158
    job simulation, 154
    role playing, 154
    video tapes, 155
    workshop, sample, outline of, 155-158

Instructional media for nongraded school, 193-213
(see also "Materials center. . . .")
Integration of subject matter into broad learning areas, 130-131
Inter-group reaction as learning technique for in-service program, 155-158
Intrinsic motivation, 214

J

Job simulation as learning technique in in-service program, 154

K

Kingsport City Schools, 96
Knowledge of nongraded programs, necessity of in planning change, 32-33

L

Language arts, teaching of in nongraded situation, 108-109
Large group instruction and team teaching, 78-79
  chart of instructional activities, 80-81
"Learning diagnostician," teacher as, 132
Learning kits, individualized, 202-203
Learning Research and Development Center at University of Pittsburgh, 26
Listening materials in materials center, 207-208
  pre-recorded lessons on tape, 207-208
  recordings, 208
Location of materials center, 198
Long range plans for team teaching, 87-93

INDEX

M

McAnnulty Elementary School as example of effective nongraded organization, 26-27
McCafferty, Mrs. Ruth, 87
McNeill Elementary School as example of effective nongraded organization, 27-28, 94, 111
Maps in materials center, 210
Materials aides, 143
Materials center for instructional media for nongraded school, 193-213
  computers and teaching machines, 203-204
  learning kits, individualized, 202-203
  maps, globes, models, modern trade books, 210-213
  multi-phased texts, 204-205
  programmed materials, 202
  questions about, 212-213
  reference texts, varied, 209
  role of, 194-195
  services provided by specialists, 193-201
    dry carrels, 196
    electronic carrels, 196
    evaluation of media, 195-196
    furniture, types of, 198
    Information Retrieval System, 201
    location, 198
    modified structures, 198
    organization of materials, 198-201
    selecting material and equipment, 195
    space, arrangement of, 196
    technical processing room, 201
  T.V. teaching, 205-206
  viewing and listening materials, 206-208
    films and filmstrips, 206-207

Materials center for instructional media for nongraded school (*Cont.*)
  viewing and listening materials (*Cont.*)
    pre-recorded lessons on tape, 207-208
    recordings, 208
    slides, opaque projections and transparencies, 207
    tachistoscope and controlled readers, 207
Materials and equipment, selection of, 195
Mathematics, teaching of in nongraded situation, 109-110
Mathematics skill sheet, model of, 165-166
Metropolitan Readiness Test, 62, 65
Microfilm reader in materials center, 201
Models in materials center, 210-211
Modified structures for greater flexibility, 198
Modules of time method in nongraded organization, 30
Motivating learner, 214-216
  recommendations for nongraded school, 215-216
Multi-cultural groups, working in, 226-228
Multi-phased texts, 204-205
Music, teaching in nongraded situation, 126

N

Narrative reporting, 174, 189-190
National Elementary Principal, 140, 140*n*, 142, 142*n*
Needs of children, diagnosing before grouping for instruction, 37-54
  (*see also* "Diagnosing children's needs. . .")
Needs never *group,* but *individual,* needs, 72

INDEX

Nelson, Senator Gaylord, 140
Nongraded Elementary School, The, 108*n*

O

Objectives of in-service program, 153-154
Observations, help from in diagnosing child's needs, 39
Opaque projections, 207
Organization of materials in materials center, 198-201
 goals, 199-201
Organizational plan for continuous progress school, model of, 70
Organizing for instruction in nongraded program, 131-132

P

Parent-teacher conferences, 174-190
 narrative reporting, 174, 189-190
Parker, Don, 202, 202*n*
Personalized process, learning as, 132
Personalized skill sheets, 161-172
 child's evaluation of independent study, 172
 for mathematics, model of, 165-166
 for reading, model of, 164
 for science, model of, 167-168
 for social studies, 170-171
Personalizing instruction in nongraded school, 214-229
 creative spark, encouraging, 220-225
  classroom atmosphere, 221-223
  humanizing curriculum, 223-225
  problems, 221
  time for creativity, providing, 223
 inquiry and experimentation, encouraging, 225-226

Personalizing instruction in nongraded school (*Cont.*)
 motivating learner, 214-216
 recommendations for nongraded school, 215-216
 multi-cultural groups, working in, 226-228
 prescribing skills needed, 216-217
 self concept, developing, 218-220
  practices, recommended, 220
 self-initiated learning, 217-218
 summary, 228-229
Persons involved in new program, evaluation of, 244
Perspectives on the Economics of Education, 142, 142*n*
Physical education, teaching of, 123-125
Physical education teacher, role of in nongraded program, 139
Pitfalls in diagnosing children's needs, 52-53
Placement of pupils, information about, 59, 60, 161, 162-163
Planning change from traditional to nongraded organization, 31-35
 Abingdon, Virginia, schools, example of, 33-35
 cooperation, broad base of, 31-32
 knowledge of nongraded programs, 32-33
 responsibility, fixing, 32
Planning sessions by principal and staff essential for successful nongraded program, 134-136
Pre-recorded lessons on tape, 207-208
Prescribing skills in personalizing nongraded school education, 216-217
Principal's role in planning nongraded program, 136-137
Problems to be solved by cooperative effort of staff, 135
Professional ethics, acquainting aide with, 150
Professional objectives for curriculum in nongraded situation, 106-108

Programmed materials for skill development, 202
Public relations, need for in developing new program, 244-251
Public relations, teacher aides and, 144-145
Pupil progress report, 173-190
  narrative reporting, 174, 189-190
  parent-teacher conferences, 174-190

Q

Questionnaire for faculty in development of new program evaluation, 235-238
Questions as criteria for evaluation of new program, 232-234
Quiet way as aid to creative thinking, 223

R

Rating scale to assess administrative change in school innovation, 239-244
Reader-primer in materials center, 201
Reading skill sheet, model of, 164
Recordings, 208
Records on continuous evaluation of pupil, 160-192
  (*see also* "Reporting practices. . .")
Reference texts, varied, in materials center, 209
Report cards in nongraded school, 173-190
  (*see also* "Reporting practices as continuous evaluation of individual pupil")
Reporting practices as continuous evaluation of individual pupil, 160-192

Reporting practices as continuous evaluation of individual pupil (*Cont.*)
  placement information, 161, 162-163
  pupil progress report, 173-190
    narrative reporting, 174, 189-190
    parent-teacher conferences, 174-190
  records, essential, 161
  skill sheets, personalized, 161-172
    child's evaluation of independent study, model of, 172
    for mathematics, model of, 165-166
    for reading, personalized, model of, 164
    for science, model of, 167-168
    for social studies, model of, 170-171
  summary, 190-192
  transfer records, 190, 191
Requirements, basic, for teacher aides, 149
Resource person, role of teacher as in nongraded program, 132-133
Responsibilities of teacher in nongraded program, 137-138
Responsibility for development of nongraded program, fixing, 32
Role playing as learning technique for in-service program, 154

S

Schedule for team teaching in nongraded plan, model of, 69, 101-105
Schooling for Individual Excellence, 202, 202n
Science, teaching of in nongraded situation, 110-111
  sample learning "packet," 111-120
Science skill sheet, model of, 167-168

INDEX

Scope and sequence, including in curriculum, 129-130
Selection of teachers in nongraded program, 137
Self concept, developing, 218-220
  practices, recommended, 220
Self-evaluation in diagnosis of child's needs, 41-44
Self-initiated learning, 217-218
Services provided by media specialists, 193-201
  dry carrels, 196
  electronic carrels, 196
  evaluation of media, 195-196
  furniture, types of, 198
  Information Retrieval System, 201
  location, 198
  materials, organization of, 198-201
    goals, 199-201
  modified structures, 198
  selecting materials and equipment, 195
  space, arrangement of, 196
  technical processing room, 201
Short range plans for team teaching, 87-93
Skill sheets, personalized, 161-172
  child's evaluation of independent study, model of, 172
  for mathematics, model of, 165-166
  for reading, model of, 164
  for science, model of, 167-168
  for social studies, model of, 170-171
Skills, personalizing nongraded schooling by prescribing, 216-217
Skills, special, for teacher aides, 149
Slides, 207
Small group instruction and team teaching, 79-82
  chart of instructional activities, 80-81
Social studies, teaching of in nongraded situation, 121-123
  skill sheet, model of, 170-171

Space in materials center, arrangement of, 196
Staff, utilizing in team approach for planning, 134-159
  community resources, 158-159
  considerations, basic, 159
  cooperative planning, 134-136
    problems, solving, 135
  in-service program for total staff, 150-158
    experiences to be included, 153
    objectives, 153-154
    techniques for learning, 154-158
    (*see also* "In service program for total staff")
  principal's role, 136-137
  specialists, using, 139-140
    arts, 139
    foreign languages, 140
    guidance counselor, 139
    physical education, 139
  summary, 159
  teacher aides, role and duties of, 140-150
    application blank, model of, 151-152
    benefits of, 148
    clerical aide, 143
    "do's and don'ts," 144
    factors causing need, 142-143
    materials aide, 143
    and public relations, 144-145
    selection of, 148-150
    (*see also* "Teacher aides, role and duties of")
    tasks for, 146-148
    teacher aide, 143
    teacher-teacher aide relations, 145-146
  teacher selection, 137
  teacher's responsibilities, 137-138
Specialists, using in nongraded program, 139-140
  (*see also* "Staff, utilizing in team approach for planning")

Staff planning for team instruction, 84-87
  guidelines, 84-87
Standard and criterion, difference between, 56
Stanford Achievement Tests, 63, 65
Structures, modified, for greater flexibility, 198
Subject matter, integration of into broad learning areas, 130-131

T

Tachistoscope, 207
"Taking Advantage of the Disadvantaged," 18n
Talents, special, for teacher aides, 149
Tape, pre-recorded lessons on, 207-208
Tasks suitable for auxiliary personnel in nongraded program, 146-148
"Teach In" as method of informing public about innovations, 250-251
Teacher, role of in nongraded program, 132-133
Teacher Aid Program Support Act of 1967, 140, 140n
Teacher aides, role and duties of, 140-150
  application blank, model of, 151-152
  benefits of, 148
  clerical aide, 143
  "do's and don'ts," 144
  factors causing need, 142-143
  materials aide, 143
  and public relations, 144-145
  selection of, 148-150
    ethics of profession, 150
    requirements, basic, 149
    talents and skills, special, 149
    volunteer aide, 150

Teacher aides, role and duties of (*Cont.*)
  tasks for, 146-148
  teacher aide, 143
  teacher-teacher aide relations, 145-146
Teacher selection, 137
Teacher's responsibilities in nongraded program, 137-138
Teacher's self image, importance of, 219-220
Teachers College Record, 18n
Teaching in a Changing World, 142n
Teaching machines in materials centers, 203-204
"Team Teaching: Is It for Me?" 75n
Team teaching approach, nongraded, 67-70
  individualization of instruction, 67-68
  organizational plan in continuous progress school, model of, 70
  schedule, model of, 69
Team teaching in nongraded structure, 73-105
  advantages of, 73-75
  definition of, 73
  disadvantages of, 75-76
  long and short range plans, 87-93
  plans, aspects of, 76-84
    chart of Tusculum View Elementary, 77
    independent study, 82-84
    large group instruction, 78-79
    leadership, 76
    small group instruction, 79-82
  schedules, model, 93-100, 101-105
  staff planning, 84-87
    guidelines, 84-87
Technical processing room in materials center, 201
Techniques for learning in in-service program, 154-158
  in-basket, 154

INDEX

Techniques for learning in in-service program (*Cont.*)
  inter-group reaction, 155-158
  job simulation, 154
  role playing, 154
  video tapes, 155
  workshop, sample, outline of, 155-158
Techniques used for evaluation of programs, 234-235
Tests, diagnostic, information from for diagnosing child's needs, 44-46
Texts, multi-phased, in materials center, 204-205
The National Elementary Principal, 140, 140*n*, 142, 142*n*
The Nongraded Elementary School, 108*n*
Time for creativity, importance of providing, 223
Torrance, E. Paul, 220*n*, 222, 222*n*
Trade books, modern in materials center, 211-213
Training for total staff in nongraded school, 150-158
  (*see also* "In-service program for total staff")
Transfer records, 190, 191
Transparencies, 207
"Turning on" students, 214-216
  recommendations for nongraded school, 215-216
Tusculum View Elementary School as example of effective nongraded organization, 28-30, 67, 96, 100, 104
T.V. teaching, 205-206

U

Underachievers, 51-52
University of Pittsburgh, 26
University of Tennessee, 28

V

Video tapes as learning technique in in-service program, 155
Viewing materials in materials center, 206-208
  controlled readers, 207
  films and filmstrips, 206-207
  slides, opaque projections and transparencies, 207
  tachistoscope, 207
Volunteer aides, 150

W

Weinstein, Gerald, 18*n*
What to teach in nongraded situation, 108-111
  arts, 125-126
  health and physical education, 123-125
  language arts, 108-109
  mathematics, 109-110
  music, 126
  science, 110-111
    sample learning "packet," 111-120
  social studies, 121-123
"Whole child" as only justifiable standard for grouping, 57
Workshop, sample of in-service, outline of, 155-158